Mohammed Adnan

Iron Does Not Rust Alone

My Journey of Growth and Strength

To my mom and dad, for your unwavering support and the life lessons that shaped my foundation; to my wife, for your endless love, sacrifice, and motivation; to my children, for being my inspiration and joy; and to my friends, for your constant encouragement and companionship. Your support and love have been my strength throughout this journey.

CONTENTS

PART I

FOUNDATIONS AND ASPIRATION

CHAPTER I

RISING FROM HUMBLE BEGINNINGS

I am deeply thankful to our Creator for blessing me with my wonderful mother (may our Creator grant her a higher place in Paradise). She has played a major role in shaping who I am today. Despite facing numerous challenges, her guidance and life lessons have been invaluable.

My mother always aspired to study further, but in her time, higher education was often not available to women. Even today, some parts of India still hold such views, though most people now complete their college education. Despite not having a formal education, my mother loved reading books and articles. Her uncle used to buy or rent books for her from the library, and she also wrote articles for monthly magazines. I believe her love for reading and writing has been passed on to me, inspiring me to write this book.

On the other hand, my father's early life was comfortable, which led him to become somewhat irresponsible. He didn't pursue higher education after school. The only negative habit was watching too many movies. Due to his health issues, my grandfather didn't pressure him to take over the family business, and because of this, the family business shut down after my grandfather passed away. As the first male child in a joint family, he received a lot of affection and special treatment from relatives.

For those unfamiliar, a joint family is where multiple generations live together in one house. My father's family lived in a house with 24 rooms, accommodating around 80 people. It was like an entire apartment complex under one roof. The beauty of a joint family is that every day feels like a festival.

However, even after many years of marriage, my father was not interested in earning and supporting our family. His bank balance, funded by my grandfather, began to decrease as we used it for our daily needs.

One evening, I overheard a heated conversation between my parents. My mother, with a mix of frustration and concern in her voice, said, "You need to start earning, for the sake of our children. How will we manage if you don't?"

My father, somewhat defensive, replied, "I know, but I just don't know where to start."

This was the reality of our situation, which led me to think. Whose mistake was this? My grandparents'? Or my father's? Or my mother's? Or the environment?

a. Was it my grandparents' fault for not guiding their child properly, blinded by their love?
b. Was it my father's fault for not realizing his responsibilities towards his wife and children?
c. Was it my mother's fault for not insisting my father start earning?
d. Was it the environment my dad grew up in, being the first-born child who always loved and supported, with every wish fulfilled?

In reality, it was a combination of the circumstances and environment of that time. My grandparents, out of love, provided a peaceful life for my father and saved money for him. However, they didn't teach him to be self-sufficient. My mother often argued, but my father's lack of responsibility was evident.

His friends moved ahead in life, but he didn't, as he wasn't willing to take any risks. Despite his flaws, my father was punctual, maintained cleanliness, and had an incredible ability to remember and follow up on tasks without any reminders. Even today, if I need to do any task tomorrow, I casually inform him about it, and he reminds me exactly at the right time.

I believe that I have inherited the best qualities from my parents. I am grateful to our Creator for blessing me with these attributes.

Eventually, all our savings were exhausted due to daily expenses. After several arguments with my mother, my father began searching for a job, marking the start of our hard times. At that time, jobs were often secured through referrals rather than through skills, education, or experience. Unlike today, there were no proper interviews.

My father got a job in a manufacturing company in our hometown, and his income was enough for our daily needs but insufficient for our education (we are 3 people, my sister, brother, & myself; I was the youngest). Relatives often helped cover our school and book fees, which affected our social status within the family.

Looking back on my life, I remember a quote: "The cycle of life: Hard times create strong men, strong men create easy times, easy times create weak men, and weak men create hard times." G. Michael Hopf

I firmly believe this quote is true. My grandfather worked hard (strong men create good times), which led to an easy life for my father (good times create weak men, and weak men create hard times). Now, I am working hard for a better future (strong men create good times). I am not saying I am a strong man; I am trying my best and working hard to give my kids a better future.

Giving love to our children is not enough. We need to educate them about right and wrong, keeping in mind that they haven't experienced much of the world and there is a generation gap. The environment in which your father went to school is different from when you were in school, and it will be entirely different when your children go to school. For example, when my father was studying, there were no computers; when I was in school, the computer revolution began; and now, my children are experiencing the era of AI and smart classrooms.

We need to adapt and respond to the current scenario. As parents, we must spend quality time with our children regularly—if not daily, then at least once or twice a week. Talk to them, play with them, understand them, teach them, help them grow, and monitor their behavior. Share your life lessons with them, and make them feel comfortable sharing their feelings with you. Especially when they are in their teens, parents must monitor their children's behavioral activities, as there are higher chances of them making wrong choices during these years.

I believe people often move in the direction where they lacked in their early life, whether it's money, love, family, or friends. For example, a person who felt unloved as a child might seek out deep, meaningful relationships as an adult. They might focus on building a loving family or forming strong friendships to create the support they didn't have growing up. This could show in their dedication to their own children or their efforts to maintain close bonds with friends.

Another example is someone who lacked a sense of belonging or strong family ties. They might spend their life creating that sense of community. They could join clubs, engage in social activities, or take on roles in community organizations to build connections they missed out on during their early years.

Similarly, someone who grew up poor might work very hard to become financially successful. They might choose high-paying jobs or start businesses, wanting to make sure they never face the same struggles again.

In short, the areas where we feel deprived in our early years often shape our goals and desires. As we grow older, we seek fulfillment and healing for those unmet needs.

Due to my early struggle with money, I developed a burning desire to earn a lot of money, and it is still not yet fulfilled. As I was still studying and my knowledge about finance was limited, my mother would often remind us, "Study hard, get good grades, and you can secure a good job and have a better life," she would say, always linking our education to the prospect of financial stability.

Although my grandfather was a businessman, given our financial situation at the time, the only viable option seemed to be pursuing a job that promised a steady and secure income. This was the perspective of our times.

Somehow, I completed my 10th grade with excellent grades. Now, the next big move in my life was selecting a course for my higher education (11th class / PUC).

During my school days, career guidance received little to no emphasis. Today, we are fortunate to have various trusts and community organizations conducting seminars and school events to guide students in pursuing higher education or choosing a college degree. Job fairs for recent graduates also help explore potential career paths. Back then, however, most students followed the flow, and the major degrees one could dream of were in Engineering, Medicine, or Arts.

From as early as the 2nd standard, I dreamed of becoming a civil engineer. I often discussed this ambition with my mother. One day, as she was cooking dinner, I asked her curiously, "Mom, what should I become when I grow up?"

She paused for a moment, then said, "You can become a doctor or an engineer." At that time, for me, engineer meant only civil engineer. Now we have multiple segments.

"Mom, what do civil engineers do?" I asked.

"They build roads, bridges, and houses," she said, stirring the pot. "They help make our cities better. And yes, they can earn well too."

"Really ? Do you think I could be one?" I asked, wide-eyed.

"Why not? But remember, it's a long journey, and it requires a lot of hard work and study," she replied, smiling at me.

Certain memories from your younger stay with you forever, and this one is one of them.

Fast forward to eight years later, and I passed my 10th grade with excellent grades, ranking among the top students in my class. My teacher, Mr. Liyaqat Ali, suggested I take up the biology group for my higher secondary education, also known as PUC. He said, "Bright students like you should consider this group, as it opens doors to many medical fields—doctors, dentists, surgeons, and even nurses."

I remember asking him, "Sir, what if I want to switch to something else later, like computers or engineering?"

He smiled and said, "That's the beauty of it. You'll have many options to choose from. But if you take up a different course now, like computer science, it might be difficult to enter the medical field later."

I'm grateful to Mr. Liyaqat Ali for his guidance. Throughout my journey, many people came and went, but few made as significant an impact as he did. My life took many different directions, experiencing numerous ups and downs on a roller coaster ride. Even though I planned every step carefully, our Creator had a different plan for me, which I will unfold as you read further. Thanks to our Creator for giving me this unique life path.

During the Physics practical exams of my 12th grade, I was confident in Math and Physics and well-prepared for the lab. I got one of the easiest questions, which only required writing the equation and process. I was happy about it. One of my classmates had brought cheat notes into the class, which is illegal. He sat in front of me, facing me, and informed me about it.

"Hey, I've got some cheat notes," my classmate whispered. "If you need any help, just let me know."

I thought to myself, "If I forget something, I can always refer to his cheat paper and complete the exam."

When I started to answer the question, I found myself blank—nothing came to mind.

"Why can't I remember anything?" I wondered. My mind was focused on the shortcut of looking at the cheat paper, preventing me from thinking deeply.

After 5-10 minutes, I leaned forward and whispered to my classmate, "Can you give me a hint for this answer?"

He nodded and whispered back, "Sure, the initial keyword is 'velocity.'"

"Thanks," I said, feeling a bit more confident. I managed to complete the exam without further help.

This reminds me of a story. You might have heard about an old man sitting in the open sky during snowfall without any cover. A businessman saw him from inside his warm house and reached out.

"Why are you sitting out here in the cold?" the businessman asked.

"I'm used to it; I don't have a home," the old man replied.

"I'll bring you some warm clothes," the businessman promised, and he went back inside but forgot.

The next morning, the businessman remembered and went to see the old man, only to find him dead with a note that read, "I was able to deal with this cold without anything, but after your words, my mindset changed, and I couldn't control myself in this cold."

Our mindset has a huge impact on how we deal with every situation and how we get influenced by other people's approaches.

When faced with challenges, a positive mindset helps us see solutions instead of obstacles. For example, during my Physics practical exam, my confidence faltered when I considered using my classmate's cheat paper. This shift in mindset caused me to blank out, revealing how easily we can be influenced by negative thoughts.

Similarly, the story of the old man in the cold illustrates how our mindset can change based on others' promises. He had managed the cold on his own, but the promise of warm clothes changed his outlook. When the promise was broken, it deeply affected him.

Surrounding ourselves with positive influences can inspire us to adopt a proactive mindset, helping us face challenges head-on. Our mindset shapes our resilience, our ability to cope with setbacks, and our drive to achieve our goals. By cultivating a positive mindset, we empower ourselves to handle life's challenges effectively and stay true to our values.

After completing my 12th grade with respectable marks, the next hurdle was preparing for entrance exams for medical and engineering courses. At that time, there were no coaching centers available in my hometown. The nearest free government coaching center was 50 km (30 miles) away. My friends and I traveled daily by train, spending hours commuting. Those train journeys became a significant part of our preparation, bonding us through shared struggles and hopes.

Despite our efforts, I did not secure a merit seat in either medical or engineering colleges. (Those who earned merit seats paid no fees or only half, with the rest covered by the government.) This was a significant setback. I tried as much as I could, putting in all my hard work, but I didn't secure the required grades. It didn't impact me a lot because I was not the most brilliant student in the class. I usually ranked within the top five in my class. None of my friends got merit seats. I thought we could take direct admissions to private medical colleges.

When we inquired about private medical college fees, we were astounded to find they ranged from 1-2 million Indian Rupees for a complete degree of 5 years (nowadays it is even more)—it is a very big amount for a family like ours. It felt like a dead end.

I lost hope of studying further, but my parents consulted with my uncle, who is well educated in our family. We then decided to consider nursing. My father and I explored a college in Chennai for a nursing course. Although the fees were lower than those for medical school, about 0.5 million Indian Rupees, it was still a substantial amount for us. Despite my father's request for a discount, the chairman remained firm on the fees and stated that no seats could be reserved due to high demand. My father thought that this was not going to happen.

We returned home, thinking that nursing was not a viable option, and decided to pursue an engineering degree instead. When we inquired at a nearby college where most of my school friends had already applied, we found that the fees were somewhat less than those for a nursing degree.

Until this time, we didn't have any savings. We hoped to secure an education loan because my marks were good, with the plan to repay it from my monthly income once I completed the degree.

The next afternoon, my mother and I visited a major bank where my father and grandfather had long-standing accounts. We were hopeful, thinking our family's history with the bank would work in our favor.

We approached the manager's desk. "Good afternoon," my mother greeted him. "We'd like to discuss a loan. My husband and his father have had accounts here for many years."

The manager checked the account details and then looked up, his expression serious. "I'm sorry, but there haven't been any recent transactions in your husband's account. We can't approve a loan without active account activity."

My heart sank. My mother said, "But our family has been banking here for decades. Doesn't that count for something?"

The manager shook his head. "Our policies require a recent transaction history to assess financial stability. Without that, we can't proceed."

My mother nodded calmly. "Thank you for your time," she said. As we left the bank, I felt the weight of disappointment.

My mother tried to convince me, "This is just a setback, not the end."

Her words reminded me that while traditions are important, we must also navigate present realities and be ready for unexpected challenges.

My dreams of becoming a doctor or working in the medical or engineering fields were shattered. My mother tried to seek help from relatives and educational trusts, but we found no support. In the meantime, two of my close friends managed to secure full and partial coverage for their entire engineering fees through a trust. When I approached the trust with my friends, they informed me that their funds were fully committed to other students.

I asked my friend, "How did you manage to get the funds?"

He replied, "We applied early, and our families knew someone in the trust. It was a bit of luck and timing, I guess."

I nodded, feeling a mix of envy and hopelessness. "I wish I had known earlier," I muttered.

Searching for these colleges took 2-3 months. Despite my passion for becoming a doctor or engineer, the lack of positive results and the heavy admission fees forced me to consider less expensive alternatives, reshaping my dreams and aspirations.

My mother motivated me by saying, "There are many successful people out there with Arts degrees. Since it is less expensive, let's approach an arts college where you can learn a computer degree for a better future." I have respect for all kinds of education and have tried to select courses that would be good for my future. However, when I applied, they informed me that the application time was over and they were no longer accepting applications.

I was not ready to give up; I informed my parents. The college principal was my father's classmate, so we went together on the same day. My father requested that the principal make an exception, but he clearly stated that we were late for this year's course and that the seats were fully occupied. He suggested selecting a different course or looking for another college, but even nearby colleges had already closed their applications.

Can you just feel this moment for a while? I studied hard, achieving excellent grades in my higher education. I passed the entrance exam, though not with merit. I tried to get a college discount but was denied. I applied for an educational loan, which was rejected. I also approached a trust, only to discover that their funds had been depleted. Finally, we tried to join an arts college but missed the application deadline. Despite our efforts, everything went in the opposite direction.

The most disheartening part was that, among all my friends, I was the only one who didn't secure admission to any college. Even today, when I think about this incident, tears come to my eyes. Life often doesn't go as planned. These setbacks, although painful, taught me resilience and determination. They reminded me that every closed door leads to a new opportunity, and it's up to us to find and walk through it.

In life, we may plan and dream, but ultimately, our Creator has a plan for us that we may not foresee. Birth and death, and our sustenance are all determined by our Creator. The trials we face, such as financial hardships and educational obstacles, are tests of our patience and faith.

My story takes a different direction, which will unfold in the next chapter.

Quranic Inspiration:

"And whoever fears Allah — He will make for him a way out and will provide for him from where he does not expect." - Surah At-Talaq (65:2-3)

Explanation: These verses and quotes resonate with my journey of rising from humble beginnings and chasing my dreams. The Quranic verse highlights the importance of faith in Allah's provision, even when the path seems uncertain. My mother's encouragement and my teachers' guidance were unexpected blessings that helped pave my way.

Motivational Quote

"The future belongs to those who believe in the beauty of their dreams." — Eleanor Roosevelt

Explanation: Eleanor Roosevelt's quote aligns with the importance of believing in one's dreams. Despite numerous obstacles, it was my belief in the beauty and possibility of my dreams that kept me motivated and striving for success.

Questions for Reflection:

1. Have you ever faced a challenging situation where you had to rely on your faith and determination to overcome it?
2. How has your environment influenced your personal growth and aspirations?
3. In what ways do you think your upbringing has shaped your goals and dreams?
4. How do you handle setbacks and keep moving forward in pursuit of your dreams?

Summary

This chapter reflects on my early life and the profound influence of my parents. Despite the challenges, my mother's unwavering dedication to our family and her love for reading and writing inspired me greatly. My father's journey was different; growing up in a comfortable environment led to a lack of responsibility, which impacted our family's financial stability. Through their stories, I learned valuable lessons about resilience and hard work.

My mother's constant encouragement and the financial struggles we faced fueled my desire to succeed and provide a better life for my family. Despite setbacks in my educational journey, including missed opportunities and financial hurdles, I remained determined to pursue my dreams. This chapter highlights the importance of a positive mindset, the impact of parental guidance, and the resilience needed to overcome life's challenges. My experiences shaped my belief that hard times create strong individuals, and I strive to embody these lessons throughout my journey.

CHAPTER 2

CHASING DREAMS

Now I was nowhere—not in college, not in a job. My brother's friends were in Chennai, a metro city in India, working in IT-related jobs. One of them suggested that I join them in Chennai for an interview the next day. At that time, BPO and call center jobs had high vacancies, and the primary requirement for a voice call center was good-spoken English. By God's grace, I managed that well. During my school days, my English teacher emphasized the importance of reading newspapers to improve our English skills. "She often said, 'Reading newspapers strengthens your reading, enhances your speaking, and deepens your understanding of the language,'".

At home, my mom encouraged the same habit. One evening, while preparing dinner, she said, "You should read the newspaper every day. It will help your English and keep you informed."

"Okay, Mom. I'll start with the sports section," I replied, knowing my love for cricket would keep me interested.

"That's a good start," she smiled. "But try reading different sections too. It will broaden your knowledge."

Following their advice, I eagerly read the sports section every morning, sharing updates like, "Did you know Sachin scored another century?" My mom would encourage me, "That's great! Now, try reading an article on current events or something inspirational."

Taking her advice, I began exploring other sections and found inspiring stories about people overcoming great odds. These stories not only motivated me, but also improved my vocabulary and comprehension.

Reading the newspaper not only kept me informed about cricket but also opened my eyes to the broader world and significantly improved my English skills.

So, on Sunday evening, I traveled with them by train and stayed in their PG (Paying Guest) accommodation for the night. The next morning, my brother's friend took me to his company for an interview. It was an open, walk-in interview, which companies usually hold for newcomers.

As we waited, I noticed the nervous energy among the 15+ people there. Some were pacing; others were rehearsing their lines. When it was my turn, I stepped forward, a bit nervous, as this was my first interview.

"What's your education?" the interviewer asked.

"I've completed my 12th grade," I replied.

He looked at me and shook his head. "From today on, we only accept college degree holders," he said. My heart sank as he rejected my application.

I waited for my brother's friend, who came out looking disappointed. "The company has changed their policy recently," he explained. "I'm sorry, I didn't know."

Feeling disheartened, I informed my parents. They tried to convince me and comfort me over the phone, saying, "Don't worry, our Creator will show us the right path. You come back home, and we will think and look together about what to do next." I traveled back home, anxiety gripping me. "What will I do now?" I thought. "I don't want to end up in a local job with no future prospects."

We started looking for other opportunities. One of my relatives mentioned that someone had opened a BPO in our hometown and offered to refer me. My mother was immediately on board. "It's a good start," she said. "You can gain experience here and move forward."

Finally, we saw a light in the darkest time of my life. It's important not to give up when faced with challenges. We need to adapt and seize the opportunities that come our way. If I hadn't accepted this BPO job, only our Creator knows what my future would have been.

We, as humans, can do any job. I have immense respect for everyone, whether they are working as a sweeper or an astronaut. There's no job that humans can't handle. Some might think that humans can't do heavy lifting, complex calculations, or that AI is replacing us. But let's not forget—it's humans who developed AI and heavy machines in the first place. At the end of the day, it's us who can do almost anything. We're now in the era of Industry 4.0, where everything is changing rapidly, and we are the driving force behind these innovations.

As Emma Watson wisely said, "Wearing unbranded and cheap clothes doesn't mean you're poor. Remember, you have a family to feed, not a community to impress." This reminds us that our worth isn't defined by appearances but by our actions and responsibilities.

Here is another thought: everyone is born with the potential to swim. Many might not know this because our parents, fearing we might drown, don't let us swim when we're infants. This fear is passed down to us, leading us to believe we can't swim. It becomes a mindset. When we finally decide to learn, we realize it's a skill that has always been within us. We just needed the opportunity and the confidence to bring it out. This applies to many areas on life—sometimes we just need to believe in our inherent abilities and give ourselves a chance to succeed.

As we navigate through life's challenges, it's essential to remain patient and adaptable.

Finally, I went for an interview at a small BPO with around 10 employees. It was more of a friendly talk than a formal process because Mr. Kamran, the owner, was a friend of my relative. He had amazing creative skills and suggested that I pursue at least a correspondence course to further my education. However, I didn't have enough money at that time to enroll in even the first year.

I informed him about our situation, and it seems our Creator had a plan. He decided to help me, possibly because I had good grades during my school years, and offered to pay for my college fees.

He recommended that I take a BBA course since it was more affordable than a BCA course, which had higher fees due to its computer-related curriculum. Despite not having a strong interest in business and accounting, I decided to pursue a BBA considering my family's financial situation. I am truly grateful to him for his help during our difficult time.

At the BPO, he first assigned me to a typing project, where we converted a scanned book into a digital Word document. I was new to typing and initially struggled with the basic home keys. My little finger couldn't press the keys properly. I practiced for multiple hours each day, even memorizing the keyboard layout while walking home from the office. After 2-3 weeks, I could type at an intermediate level.

It was during Ramadan, and we worked on the typing project at night. After night prayers, we started typing from 10 PM to 4 AM, stopping for Suhoor. Working night shifts was challenging but also fun. Later, he asked me to learn about computer hardware—hard drives, RAM, processors, and how to install software and applications. Before joining this BPO, I had zero computer knowledge. I only went to cyber cafes to play video games. I studied biology, so I had no computer education. Thanks to our Creator and Mr. Kamran for providing me with the opportunity to learn. These were difficult concepts for me at first, but I was determined to learn.

I made many mistakes during the learning process, like installing the wrong software, forgetting the names of hardware components, or applying the wrong method, which broke the software, and we had to reinstall everything. I felt frustrated and doubted my abilities, but I practiced and worked hard to remember things. My love for computer technology started at this office.

The company was also working on a software application for the manufacturing industry using VB6 and SQL, and they encouraged me to learn programming as well. Within six months, I developed a strong interest in computer technology and programming. Although I couldn't get an engineering degree, I was fortunate to have the opportunity to learn programming skills on the job.

My boss appointed two new candidates and asked me to train them in hardware and software. I was a short-tempered guy back then and felt a lot of pressure to ensure they learned quickly and correctly. One of the trainees was a local football player. My strictness and impatience led him to leave the job, and I felt terrible about it. It weighed heavily on my conscience, making me realize that my approach was too harsh and unkind. Looking back, I realize I could have approached the situation differently. Now, I am a different person; obviously, having many years of experience has taught me many life lessons.

Despite being a startup and with me still learning, the salary was very minimal. At the same time, my uncle's brother-in-law, who managed a tannery (a leather manufacturing company), mentioned he needed someone for planning work. I was torn between staying in a job I loved and pursuing a new opportunity that promised better financial stability.

Quranic Inspiration:

"Indeed, with hardship [will be] ease." (Quran 94:6)

These verses and quotes reflect my journey through unexpected turns and the discovery of my true path. The Quranic verse assures us that ease follows hardship. When my initial plans to secure a college seat fell through, I felt lost. However, this hardship led me to unexpected opportunities, such as the BPO job, which became a stepping stone in my career.

Motivational Quote

"Our greatest glory is not in never falling, but in rising every time we fall." — Confucius

Explanation: This quote perfectly encapsulates my experiences in these chapters. Despite the setbacks and failures, what truly mattered was my ability to rise again and keep moving forward. It's a powerful message that encourages resilience and determination in the face of adversity.

Questions for Reflection:

1. What dreams or goals did you have as a child, and how have they changed over time?
2. How do you stay motivated when pursuing a long-term goal that requires hard work and dedication?
3. Have you ever faced pressure from others to choose a particular career path? How did you handle it?
4. How do you balance following your passion with practical considerations, such as financial stability?

Summary

I found myself without a college admission or a job. My brother's friends in Chennai suggested trying for a BPO job due to my strong English skills, a habit I picked up from reading newspapers, as my mother encouraged. Despite my efforts, I was turned down because I lacked a college degree. Feeling disheartened, I returned home but kept searching for opportunities. Eventually, a relative referred me to a small BPO in our hometown. Mr. Kamran, the owner, not only gave me a job but also covered my college fees, enabling me to pursue a BBA despite our financial constraints.

At the BPO, I started from scratch, learning typing, computer hardware, and software skills. Despite initial struggles and mistakes, I persevered through night shifts during Ramadan, gradually mastering the tasks. My love for computer technology grew during this time, leading me to explore programming. Eventually, a new opportunity arose in a tannery, forcing me to choose between financial stability and my passion for technology. This chapter highlights the importance of resilience, adaptability, and seizing opportunities despite setbacks.

PART 2

NAVIGATING EARLY CAREER

CHAPTER 3

THE UNEXPECTED TURN

My parents wanted me to accept a new job opportunity for a higher, more stable income and a chance to learn many new things. Although it required giving up my passion for programming to support my family, I understood the importance of putting their needs first. As I grew older and took on more responsibility for my family, I began to understand our situation more deeply. Since then, I've always put my family first, even above my own wishes or choosing a company. I believed that one day I would get a chance to start programming again and fulfill all my dreams.

Whenever I had to choose between my personal goals and my family's needs, I always chose my family. This belief kept me hopeful that, with patience and perseverance, I could achieve both personal and professional success without compromising my family's well-being. I accepted the new job and notified Mr. Kamran, leaving the company immediately because the role was only a six-month training period.

The next day, I began my journey by bus. Traveling wasn't a common activity for us back then. We rarely traveled except during the school summer holidays, when we visited relatives and played with cousins. We didn't even care about the time and weather; we played a lot of cricket until we got tired. Future generations will not experience these events. We are lucky to have been born in that generation, and we thank to our Creator for blessing us with such memorable moments.

Nowadays, holidays often involve foreign or national trips to cool or adventurous places. Times have changed a lot since my childhood, as you will feel throughout this book.

I boarded the bus from my town, needing to travel about 5 kilometers. I didn't know the route, and I didn't have a bike. I asked the bus conductor to inform me when my stop arrived. However, I became confused by the village names. Let's call them Small Town and Big Town for simplicity. The conductor said we had reached Big Town, but I assumed we would pass Small Town first. I got off the bus.

"Excuse me," I said, approaching a local. "I'm looking for a company that lies between Small Town and Big Town. Am I on the right path?"

The elderly man smiled kindly and said, "Big Town comes first and then Small Town, but you're close. Just walk a bit further, and you'll see it on your right."

After walking a little further, I started feeling hopeless. I thought of returning home, but my heart pushed me to continue. Finally, I found the company after walking for nearly half a kilometer.

In the early 2000s, applying for entry-level positions often depended on referrals. My father advised me to maintain a positive attitude during the interview. If asked about my familiarity with various applications, he said, "Just say you know them." During the interview, when asked about my knowledge of Microsoft Office and Photoshop, I confidently said, "Yes, Sir, I have utilized these applications in my previous role."

After sharing details about my family, the interviewer, who knew my uncle, offered me the position. Not wanting to miss the opportunity, I eagerly agreed to start immediately. That was it—my interview was complete, and I had a new job. I felt very happy.

Times have changed, and so have interview processes. Today, even freshers go through multiple rounds of interviews, and only the top candidates are selected. You need to be well-prepared and knowledgeable about the position you are applying for.

This was my first big company with over 500 employees. I was part of the planning team, responsible for communicating with customers and following up with the production team for shipments at a leather manufacturing company.

As I said earlier, I knew only the basics of Excel, but I was good at typing, which I learned in the previous startup. My boss asked me to update daily records in Excel, which they used for data entry and reporting. During that time, there wasn't much software like Microsoft Dynamics, SAP, or Oracle. Excel was everywhere, and even today, people use it extensively.

I was a fresher and didn't know much about the manufacturing process or job responsibilities. I made many mistakes, which doubled my boss's workload as he had to teach and review my work. For me, my mistakes were reasonable because I needed time to understand the process. After a month, he complained to the manager about my work. The manager called to warn me that if I didn't improved within the next month, I would be terminated.

Every day felt like I was walking on thorns. My boss was constantly frustrated with my work and complained to others. One day, Mr. Ali from another department noticed my struggles and said to my boss, "Remember, you were new once too. It takes time to learn the ropes."

My parents were my biggest supporters during this tough time, especially my mother. She would say, "Give it a month. If things don't improve, we can look for another job." Her words really boosted my morale.

I started working late, often until 7 or 8 PM, to understand the work better. I asked colleagues for help to understand the processes and worked hard to improve my mistakes. Gradually, I took on more responsibilities, which allowed my boss to relax and go home early.

One day, the manager called me into his office. "I've noticed your progress," he said. "Keep up the good work." Hearing that made me really happy.

My usual day at the office began by turning on my computer, which was really slow. It took almost half an hour to open the big Excel file with multiple calculations. Then, I would go to the production department to note the status of every order, update the Excel report, and inform the manager.

"Assalamu alaikum, Amjad Bhai," I greeted the production supervisor as I walked into the department. "How's the order for the new client coming along?"

Amjad Bhai looked up from his papers and smiled. "Walaikum assalam, it's going well. Just a few more hours, and we should be good to go. How's the planning team holding up?"

"We're getting there," I replied, noting down the updates. "Learning new things every day."

He was one of my biggest supporters.

My boss would take this information and report it to the client and the Managing Director of the company.

While taking the order status, I had to visit every department during the first hour of the day. I greeted other staff members and had casual chats with them, returning to my desk after 45 minutes to an hour. I would then update the Excel file within an hour and start exploring additional Excel features, such as advanced formulas, shortcuts, and VBA controls. Since IT has restricted internet access, I relied on Excel's help feature to learn (thanks to Microsoft for this amazing tool and tutorial within Microsoft Excel).

By learning these things, I created another Excel file in parallel, which worked faster than the old one. After testing it for a few days, I discussed it with my boss. He was very happy because it saved time and was neatly formatted as per the Managing Director's guidelines.

Similarly, I created and enhanced many reports that significantly increased our productivity. As word spread about my improvements, people from other departments that relied heavily on Excel began to approach me for help.

I took on each request with enthusiasm, dedicating my time and skills to reducing their workload wherever possible. This not only helped my colleagues but also fostered a collaborative environment where we all supported each other's success. The sense of accomplishment I felt from making a positive impact on their daily tasks was incredibly rewarding.

I didn't waste my free time. Instead, I tried to remember Excel shortcuts by repeating the same steps, which I still use today. Thanks to my boss, who insisted I stay at my desk even if I didn't have work, because it gave a bad impression in front of the manager. If someone was seen roaming around, it meant they didn't have much work, which could lead to a bad impression, more responsibilities, or even termination. I used those hours to learn and relearn.

I was performing well at work, with my daily tasks involving detailed planning and constant communication with various departments. Ensuring that customer orders were processed efficiently required constant attention to detail. I had enough money to pay for my second and third years of college, and the management was kind enough to allow me to attend classes during the weekends. College classes were usually held on Saturday and Sunday. At my job, we worked six days a week, unlike the typical five-day work week in the IT industry or some other industries.

After gaining two years of experience, I noticed the increment was very low. My parents started comparing my salary with others who had similar experience. This is something typical Indian parents do. "Wo dekho Khanna Saheb ka beta kitna kama raha hai... Look at Khanna's son; he earns a lot."

My brother had started working after his 12th grade due to our family situation, so he knew many people around town. One of his colleagues informed him about a vacancy in costing department at a company later acquired by a German brand.

I went there one afternoon for an interview with my resume. My boss, Mr. Hussain, interviewed me. It wasn't very technical, but it involved a lot of Excel work. Over the last two years, I had practiced Excel extensively. I shared my work experience with him, and he agreed. The package they offered me was three times what I was getting at my current job.

I came back home happily and informed my parents. "Mom, Dad, the interview went well, and I got the new job! They're offering me three times my current salary," I exclaimed.

My mother smiled and said, "That's wonderful! We knew you could do it."

My father added, "You made the right choice. Stay focused and give it your best."

The next day, I submitted my resignation letter. My current employer was shocked and initially didn't accept it. They offered to double my salary, but I had already decided to join the new company and stayed firm in my decision. Eventually, they agreed to relieve me, and I joined the new company.

On the first day of the job, they introduced me to the office as usual, and I got a knowledge transfer session from a lady who was leaving due to family issues. I started to work on the costing project, and to my surprise, the new boss was actually the head of IT in that company. He was developing in-house software applications using VB6 and SQL, which I loved doing. Although it was not within my scope of work, I saw potential opportunities in the future to practice and maybe even contribute.

My boss had impressive programming skills and over 10 years of experience. One day, I asked him, "With your skills, why are you here? You could join any big IT company and earn a lot more. In manufacturing, software isn't the main revenue source. The management invests more in products that in IT, resulting in lower salaries for IT staff compared to those in manufacturing. But in IT, it's their core business, and the pay is better."

He smiled and said, "It's my father's advice. He always said that we should serve the place where we were born and raised. That's why I'm working here in our hometown."

His words struck me. Many people go abroad to study or earn more to support their families. But here was someone with a different perspective, choosing to give back to his roots. It made me think deeply about my own choices and the value of serving our community.

Unfortunately for the company, but fortunately for me, after two months of my joining, the company, which was a joint venture between an Indian and a German company, decided to separate their businesses. Hence, the whole company was taken over by the German company, and the employee split started. My boss, who had been with the company for 10 years, was the head of IT. The Indian owner asked him to join his new company in the next building within the same compound and to hand over his responsibilities to someone else.

My boss respected the owner's decision and asked if I could take over the department and the software application, as he knew that I had little experience in software application development and computer hardware. Inside, I felt like "mann me laddu phoot rahe hain" (my heart was bursting with joy). Outside, I initially hesitated to accept, but I knew if I missed this chance, someone else would take over, and my dream of developing software would slip away. So, I accepted, and he did the knowledge transfer. As he was in the next building and easily reachable, he really helped me a lot, even after the split, clarifying my doubts about the application.

My parents were also pleased because such opportunities are rare, and we need to seize them as soon as they arise.

I worked very hard on this, studying the coding even late at night to understand how the application and the process of the company worked. Now, I had more responsibility for managing both software and hardware and the department. I appointed someone and transferred my previous job responsibilities to him due to the change in my role.

I was thrilled to be earning three times my previous salary, working at a job I loved, advancing in my position, and finally completing my BBA degree. Good things come to those who believe in our Creator and wait.

Hadith Inspiration:

"The Prophet Muhammad (peace be upon him) said: 'Allah does not burden a soul beyond that it can bear...'" - Sahih Bukhar

Explanation: The hadith reminds us that we are never burdened beyond our capacity. Despite feeling overwhelmed by my new responsibilities, I trusted that I could handle them. This belief helped me stay resilient and eventually excel in my role.

Motivational Quote:

"Challenges are what make life interesting and overcoming them is what makes life meaningful." –

Joshua J. Marine

Explanation: Joshua J. Marine's quote underscores the importance of facing and overcoming challenges. The journey of learning and mastering Excel and managing a team not only made my life more interesting but also brought a deep sense of accomplishment.

Questions for Reflection:

1. Have you ever faced a sudden change in your life that required you to adapt quickly?
2. How do you maintain a positive mindset when dealing with unexpected challenges?
3. What role do you think your mindset plays in overcoming difficulties?
4. How do you approach new opportunities that come your way, even if they seem risky or uncertain?

Summary

In this chapter, my parents urged me to take a new job for better income and growth, even though it meant giving up my passion for programming. I accepted, prioritizing my family's needs over my personal goals. This taught me to always put my family first, hoping to return to programming someday.

Navigating unfamiliar routes, I started my new job in the planning team of a large company. Initially, I struggled with Excel and faced the threat of termination. However, by working late, enhancing my skills, and gaining recognition for my efforts, I received a significant salary increase and took on new responsibilities.

I then secured a better job with a higher salary, discovering opportunities in software development. Inspired by my boss, who chose to serve his hometown, I embraced this new role. When the company split, I was given the opportunity to lead the IT department, which allowed me to combine my passion for software and hardware. This opportunity was a turning point, allowing me to pursue my passion while supporting my family.

CHAPTER 4

DISCOVERING MY PATH

I was working as usual in my regular job, writing lots of code to build applications, managing hardware and databases, and handling management reporting. Eager to take on more responsibilities, learn, advance, and grow quickly, I had been searching for an IT job. I prepared my resume and posted it on various job portals. I got a call from a big company in India and scheduled an offline interview in Chennai. I gave a fake reason to my manager and took leave to attend the interview. Since I rarely took many leaves, he accepted my request without much questioning.

I prepared all the required documents and traveled early in the morning by bus to be on time. I had a light breakfast after arriving there and went to the interview location punctually.

I saw over 100 candidates present for various job roles. Being an introvert, I initially hesitated to communicate with people. As I waited for the HR team to call me, I noticed a few resumes from others who had come for the same interview. Their certification provided them with an additional advantage. I didn't have any certifications. Learning again even after school and college had always been somewhat boring, but now, years later, I realize that learning and getting certified are crucial as we progress with new and emerging technologies. As an example, Nokia didn't do anything wrong, but they didn't adapt to the changing world, so they fell from the top position in the mobile market.

The interviewer asked me a few questions. "So, can you explain your experience with SQL databases?" the interviewer asked.

"Well, I handle databases daily," I stammered. "But articulating the specifics is challenging right now."

He smiled encouragingly. "Let's focus on practical scenarios then."

Even though I was working on these tasks daily, I didn't know how to answer them properly. I didn't manage to answer many of his questions.

He mentioned there would be another round, a group discussion, and then an HR round. Since there were over 100 candidates that day, the HR teams couldn't manage all the rounds. In the evening, they informed everyone that they would call us for the next round if selected and asked us to leave for the day.

I wasn't sure about my performance, so I returned home. Back then, if they said that they would call you, it usually meant you were rejected.

A few days later, I got a call from the company. The person said they had a backdoor process (offering the job directly without completing the interview) and could give me a job in that role. He asked for 30,000 Indian Rupees, which was a significant amount for me in 2007. I asked Mr. Matheen, one of my well-wishers, for advice. He said these kinds of calls, especially when they ask for money upfront, are scams. I informed the HR person that I couldn't afford it as I was a poor guy. He finally asked for 5,000 rupees for further processing. I thought this was not a big amount compared to 30,000, so I agreed. Again, I clarified with Mr. Matheen, and he advised me to check if it was a scam and suggested doing a bank transfer. The person refused and asked me to deliver the money in person rather than via bank transfer, as he feared being caught with counterfeit bills.

I informed my mother about the whole story, and she said it would be good if I got this job as this was from the IT industry, which was my ultimate goal and one of the top 3 companies in India during that time.

I couldn't take another leave because I had just taken one for the interview a few days earlier, so I traveled in the evening after office hours and reached another destination at the Chennai Bus Stand. Over the phone, he instructed me to hand over the money to another person. That person came, took the money from me, and left without any further communication. Smartphones were not common during that time, and I couldn't talk with him. He disappeared quickly into the crowd. And I returned home early in the morning, at 6 AM as the travel time is 4 hours from my town.

I informed my parents of the situation. They also believed that it was a scam.

I followed up with him over the phone regarding the offer letter, and a few days later, I received the appointment letter via email. I was so excited that I had finally gotten a job in the IT industry. A dream had come true. I informed my parents and Mr. Matheen. They were also happy to know that it wasn't a scam.

I didn't resign from my current company. Instead, I thought to work for a few more days and then get permission from the new company for a few days to properly hand over my projects to the existing company.

I went to the specified place mentioned in the appointment letter. Since there were over 100 candidates during the job interview, many people were also present on the first day. When I got to the reception with the appointment letter, the receptionist checked my name against a list and couldn't find it. She then turned to me and said that I had been scammed. This job application was fake, and like me, many others had also been scammed. I was shattered and requested that she take the interview now and, based on that, give me a job. She clearly said it was not possible. They were collecting handwritten letters from the candidates to report to the police. I also wrote down all the details and handed them over to her. When I tried to call the person who had taken the money, the phone was switched off.

I returned home sadly. My parents gave me hope, saying that everything would be fine. My sadness was not just because of the job loss but mainly due to being scammed out of money. I tried to call him for many months afterward, but there was no reply. I tried other numbers; when he heard my voice and story, he disconnected the call, and thereafter, he didn't answer any of my calls.

This story is from 2007. Even today, fraud occurs frequently through various methods. Committing fraud is not permissible in any religion. Even knowing it's a scam, people still create businesses around this idea. I don't know how these people can sleep after taking hard-earned money from others.

Even in our personal communication or financial transactions, we need to keep track of or have a written agreement for better mutual understanding between parties. I mean between you and the other person.

One of the good decisions I made during this time was not to quit my current company. There were no rules regarding the notice period at that time. If I had informed them about it, then I would have been jobless. Thanks to our Creator for saving me from such difficulties.

After this, I began working hard at my current company. The major improvement I made here is that in building the complete software from scratch with the new technologies of that time, my close friend Niaz, a Software Engineer, helped me a lot during the initial learning of new technologies. I worked day and night, often staying up until 2 AM. It wasn't because of the workload, but because of my passion for building software applications. The main reason was that developing something that could reduce others' workload or save their time gave me immense satisfaction. Knowing that I could make a positive impact on others' lives through my software was incredibly fulfilling. I used to sit with the users and understand their pain points, keeping in mind standard practices, management rules, users' benefits, and software limitations. I tried my best to build smooth software.

I completed the in-house application within six months and successfully implemented it. The CEO (Mr. Ahad Basha) appreciated my efforts and awarded me an appreciation letter, similar to an "Employee of the

Year" award. I continued working there for the next four years until another surprise came my way...

After the first IT job scam in 2007, I continued working diligently and received promotions, eventually becoming the MIS (Management Information System) in charge. I was happy with my progress.

My CEO (Mr. Ahad Basha) used to say that he was learning new things every day. At nearly 50 years old, he still had this drive to keep learning. At that time, I had just started my career, and I wondered how someone at his stage could still be learning daily. It didn't make sense to me back then. But as I progressed in my own career, I began to understand what he meant. He was right—there is no end to learning. If you have the will, you can learn anything—at any time and about any subject—whether it's related to your profession, personal life, or social interactions. This realization has been one of the most valuable lessons in my journey. Keep learning and making an impact.

In 2011, I got an opportunity to visit Germany for an official project. When I informed my mom, she was on cloud nine. She had always dreamed of sending me abroad to work. Even though it was for a short time, at least her dream came true. She informed all her relatives, and they were shocked to hear that the company was bearing all the expenses. This was not normal during that time, especially in my hometown industry. Thanks to the owner (Mr. Christof Bär) for the opportunity.

I went to Germany for three weeks. It was also the first time I sat on an airplane in my life, and it was a long, nonstop 10-hour Emirates flight. It was a really amazing journey. When I arrived, it was a beautiful 3 to 4 degrees Celsius in the morning around 8 AM.

I was picked up by an Indian driver—a nice person. I felt very happy to see an Indian in another country.

I went to the office and introduced myself to everyone. They were nice people, and we had official training. Lunch was provided within the company for all staff. One thing I badly missed was our Indian food. We generally used to use spices, but here they rarely do. One dish that was strange to me was the lunch they served, which consisted of big leaves—bigger than spinach leaves—plus boiled salted, potatoes. Can you believe us Indians are having this for lunch? I believe it is never Indian food. I ate that, and it wasn't bad. Their pancakes were amazingly soft and delicious.

I wish I could celebrate some festivals there. Luckily, it was Halloween time, and I didn't know much about it. While we were staying at the house, someone rang the bell, and I was alone at the time. Generally, we stayed with three colleagues in that house.

When I opened the door, three kids around 6-10 years old, dressed in different costumes, shouted, "Happy Halloween!" I smiled and greeted them, but they were looking at me silently. I didn't know why. There was also a woman with them. I informed her that I didn't know about this festival and asked if I needed to give something. She replied, "Yes, some gifts or sweets." During my stay, I purchased some chocolates to take home for my family and relatives. I picked some and shared them with the kids. They were happy and moved to the next house.

On weekends, I would get recommendations for nearby tourist spot from my colleagues, then visit them by bus and return afterward. It was a beautiful experience, and I got the opportunity to interact with people from multiple different cultures. The cleanliness and how they kept their places were really beautiful.

If I travel to any new places, I usually forget the route. In my hometown, friends used to guide me. As I was alone in Germany and smartphones were not common, I took lots of selfies and location photos with a digital camera. Whenever I had doubts, I referred to those images and returned the same way.

The first week, I was eager to look at new places and focused fully on office work. The second week, I got a little bored and thought about when I would return to my hometown. During the third week, I was happy and purchased gifts and chocolates for my family members and relatives.

Daily, I used to call back home from the office to greet them and check on their status. My mom was worried about me, as it was my first time traveling abroad and living without family. On the last day in Germany, I informed my mom to bring some Indian food to taste the Indian spices.

My mom brought the whole family and my sister's family to the airport. It was a grand welcome for me.

They brought paratha and khorma (gravy). The taste was amazing for me, perhaps because I had tasted it after three weeks. On the way back home, I shared all my experiences with my family.

Overall, it was a great experience.

I returned to the India office, installed the software, trained our staff, and successfully implemented it. It was an additional workload for the staff, but they managed as it was the management's decision.

During this time, I was fortunate to work with a supportive team. We built great memories together, especially during public holidays when we traveled to tourist destinations. These trips were not just a break from work but also opportunities to bond and create lasting friendships. These experiences provided much-needed relief and joy amidst the challenges, reminding me that even during tough times, there are moments of happiness and friendship.

At that time, working abroad, especially in Gulf countries, was a popular trend. Many people aimed to work there for a few years, save money, and return home to settle down with a good bank balance.

As you know from my earlier chapters, this was one of my mother's dreams. She believed that if I worked abroad, we could have a good house and a happy future. My cousins were already working abroad and saving a significant amount. My aunt informed my mother about their success, and from then on, my mother started pushing me to leave my job.

"Son, just think about the future," my mother urged. "If you go abroad now, we can have a better life and a secure future."

"I understand, Mom," I replied. "Let's see what opportunities come our way."

I shared this plan with my close office colleagues. Not all colleagues are friends, but the cashier, Afzal, was one of my close colleagues. We had a good bond during those days. He was married with two kids and was also looking for an opportunity abroad for a better future. Salaries in our hometown were not good at that time, though they are better now. One staff member in our accounts department, Akbar, had returned from Saudi due to family issues. He was also trying to return to Saudi for a better package.

Akbar reached out to his contacts and explained that three of us were looking for jobs abroad—two for accounting (Akbar and Afzal) and one for computer hardware (me). One of his contacts asked us to come for an interview in Bangalore. We traveled by train and attended the interview at a construction tile showroom. They had a branch in Saudi and were looking for candidates from our town or nearby areas.

The interview was not very technical, just at a high level. They said they would reply to Akbar for further updates. Usually, when they say they will update you later, it often means there is no opportunity, as that "later" never comes—it's an indirect way of saying no.

We returned home without much expectation and continued working at our current jobs. After a few days, they asked us to send our passport details and informed us to be ready to leave within a week once the visa arrived. The package offered was good compared to our current salaries.

By this time, our company had adopted a notice period policy. We needed to resign and transfer our knowledge to our successors within 30 days to clear our PF (Provident Fund) and gratuity.

Afzal and I asked Akbar for the confirmation about the job, as we hadn't received it yet and needed to leave within a week after obtaining the visa. He assured us that the owner was a good guy who wouldn't commit fraud, so we could resign and wait for the visa.

We all three resigned within a week but didn't file on the same day to avoid suspicion. Even after submitting our resignations within a week, our management understood that we were planning something.

My CEO (Mr. Ahad Basha) called me and asked about it. I lied and said that I got an opportunity at an IT company, linking it with the fake job I had been scammed for a few years back.

As the days passed, Afzal and I grew nervous about whether we would get the visa. Akbar tried to reach them multiple times but received no response. I even got the owner's number and spoke with him directly. He assured me that he was working on it and would get the visa very soon.

Meanwhile, I received an email from the managing director of my company requesting that I stay until his visit next month, so we could discuss the possibility of my retention. I was happy to work abroad, so I replied that I had decided to pursue opportunities outside the company and couldn't stay back.

Thirty days passed, and all handovers were done. I returned home jobless. There was no response from the new job owner. A week later, Akbar got his visa and went to Saudi, leaving Afzal and me jobless.

Each day without a job felt like a heavy weight on my shoulders. My parents tried to hide their worry, but I could see the concern in their eyes. Although my brother and father earned, the majority of my contribution came from me. Going abroad wasn't solely my decision—it was a joint family decision. We approached other jobs locally and abroad but had no success.

Twenty days passed without a job. Each passing day was hard. My family depended on my salary, and I couldn't sit idle. Despite their support, the pressure was mounting, and I felt the burden of being the primary breadwinner.

We say that "mashwara" is the best thing when making decisions. It means taking input and suggestions from parents, friends, siblings, etc., depending on the situation. This has a positive impact, and even if something goes wrong, they will still support you.

If, even after making a mutual decision, things don't go your way, believe that something good is going to happen. Whatever we plan, our Creator is the greatest planner of all. Our Creator will not let anyone go down. Have faith that everything that has happened and everything that will happen is for the best.

This situation reminds me of my ex-colleague Attaullah Bhai's dialogue: "Adnan, if someone wants to leave the company but his provision (rizq) is destined to come from this company, then he cannot go away from this company. On the contrary, if you want to stay in the company but your provision (rizq) has ended in your destiny, then you cannot stay here." The same happened to me. My provision (rizq) stopped at my previous company for a reason, and I came out of there.

While searching for a job as a programmer and hardware specialist, I networked with similar people in the field. Mr. Matheen informed me that there was a vacancy at a top company in my hometown. I was very excited because the position and package were really good. I didn't want to miss this opportunity.

I went for an interview, and as usual, they asked me about my experience. Surprisingly, they didn't ask any technical questions. One of the interviewers leaned forward and said, "Can you show us something as proof of your work?" I felt a bit nervous. I wasn't technically sound, and my degree wasn't related to software. But I had my laptop with me, which had the software I worked on installed.

"Sure," I said, opening my laptop. "I have two projects here. One is our own product, Dewdrops, and the other is a project I developed at my previous company, with dummy data."

I started by showing them Dewdrops, explaining the features and functionalities I had worked on. They seemed impressed. I then transitioned to the next project, outlining my role and its impact. The interviewers nodded and exchanged approving glances.

After I finished, one of them said, "This is good work. Thank you for sharing it with us."

I felt a wave of relief wash over me. The interview ended on a positive note, and I returned home happily, feeling confident about my chances.

That evening, I got a call from Mr. Matheen. He asked how the interview went. I explained everything, and he was upset. He advised me that what I had done was wrong—a kind of security breach. I should not have given a demo of the software application. If they wanted to validate me, they should have asked questions. Even if they asked to see the software, I should not have shown it because it was another company's product. Now they rejected me because they suspected I might steal their application and demo it to other companies if they hired me. This created a bad impression of my image.

My dreams shattered. I felt bad about myself. I hadn't learned technical skills even during my jobless days. One reason was the lack of internet access. At that time, only companies had reliable internet. We didn't have smartphones, 4G/5G internet, or ChatGPT-like technology. Learning had to be done either in the company or at a Cyber Café.

This situation reminds me of a dialogue with my friend and former colleague, Mr. Afzal. He used to say, "Karna to raaste hazaar, nakarna to bahane hazaar," which means, "If you truly want to achieve something, you'll find a thousand ways. If not, you'll just find a thousand excuses."

Afzal continued, "On the other hand, if you're not fully committed, you'll find a thousand excuses to avoid taking action. It's easy to focus on reasons why something can't be done. But remember, those are just excuses. The key is to focus on the solutions, not the problems."

His advice made me realize that self-belief is crucial. If you don't believe in yourself, who else will? Motivation must come from within. Afzal's words served as a constant reminder that our mindset plays a significant role in our success.

One evening, I sat down with my parents and discussed the challenges. "Don't lose hope," my mother said gently. "We believe in you, and something good will come your way."

My father nodded in agreement, adding, "Just keep trying, and don't give up."

Our parents, siblings, friends, and colleagues can inspire us, but the real spark needs to come from within us. We have to feel that burning desire to achieve something—whether it's landing a job, creating a product, or learning new skills. Success is the result of hard work; it doesn't come for free.

Success looks different for everyone. For some, it's about becoming a millionaire. For others, it's buying a house, mastering new skills, making a positive impact on society, or even becoming the Prime Minister. Each person's idea of success is unique, but the common factor is the effort and determination put into reaching those goals.

No matter what your dream is, the key is to keep pushing forward and working hard. Inspiration from others can guide us, but our own drive is what will ultimately lead us to success.

If you win in your thoughts, you will also win in real life. If you believe in yourself and have a positive mindset, you're already halfway to success. Your thoughts shape your actions, so if you think you can achieve something, you're more likely to make it happen. Winning in your mind means having confidence and determination, which help you overcome obstacles and achieve your goals in real life.

Finally, I informed my previous company's General Manager, Abdul Razak, who was also my friend. His life journey really inspired me (I believe it requires an entire book to capture his amazing life journey). Although we were good friends, I hadn't informed him about this earlier. After hearing my story, he was worried about me. A few days later, he asked me to attend an interview in a nearby town, 16 km from my home.

I went there, and the owners were good. They gave me a job that wasn't related to my previous work. I was a software programmer and hardware specialist, but they offered me a production planning and marketing job. The package was less than my previous salary.

I came back home and informed my parents. They said that being employed is better than being jobless. Many people change careers and travel long distances daily to earn an income, so why not accept this offer and start tomorrow?

"We tried to go abroad, but it didn't happen. Your provision (rizq) from the previous company has ended. Now, our Creator has given you a chance to go in a different direction. Who knows? This job might be life-changing for you. Remember, things don't always go our way. Sometimes it's hard, but we need to adjust and move forward. Keep praying and have faith in our Creator," my mother advised.

Finally, I thought about it and decided to take the job. The journey with this company was interesting and brought out a different side of me, which we will discuss in the next chapter.

Quranic Inspiration:

"And whoever fears Allah — He will make for him a way out. And will provide for him from where he does not expect." (Quran 65:2-3)

Explanation: This verse reassures us that by maintaining faith and fear of Allah, even in the most challenging times, a way out will emerge from unexpected places. Throughout my journey, from facing job scams to finding new opportunities and managing new responsibilities, my faith in Allah's plan helped me overcome these challenges. It's a reminder that trust in Allah brings solutions from the most unexpected sources.

Motivational Quote:

"The only limit to our realization of tomorrow is our doubts of today." — Franklin D. Roosevelt

Explanation: This quote resonates with experiences of doubt and uncertainty during my job transitions and challenges. It highlights the importance of overcoming self-doubt to achieve future success. By pushing through my doubts, I was able to find new opportunities and grow in my career.

Questions for Reflection:

1. How do you respond to new opportunities that are outside your comfort zone?
2. Have you ever taken on a role or responsibility that was different from what you originally planned? How did it turn out?
3. What skills have you developed that you didn't initially expect to learn?
4. How do you handle situations where you need to adapt to new challenges quickly?

Summary

In this chapter, I remained committed to my regular job while actively seeking growth in the IT field. I attended an interview in Chennai, which didn't go well. Later, I received a scam call offering a backdoor job for a fee. Despite my skepticism, I paid a smaller amount but discovered it was a scam upon arrival.

Grateful I hadn't quit my current job; I continued working hard, developing new software, and earning recognition. A significant opportunity arose when I was sent to Germany for a project, fulfilling my mother's dream of seeing me work abroad. This experience taught me the importance of continuous learning, a lesson my CEO (Mr. Ahad Basha) often emphasized.

Despite setbacks, including a failed attempt to secure a job abroad, my family's support kept me resilient. Eventually, I secured a new job that wasn't in my field but offered stability. This chapter highlights the value of adaptability and seizing opportunities, leading to a fulfilling career path.

PART 3

PROFESSIONAL GROWTH AND CHALLENGES

CHAPTER 5

OVERCOMING CHALLENGES

This company changed my perspective on working direction. Before this job, I was a software guy focused on handling software implementation and developing new applications for users. During my interview with the management and the company owner, I clearly expressed my preference for software development. While they had no issues with it, their primary focus was on production, planning, and merchandising. Although I had some knowledge in those areas, it was still new to me.

They had over 100 employees, but in terms of technology, they had not yet evolved. Everything was maintained using Microsoft Excel. I started to understand their process and initiated improvements in their existing Excel system.

On the other hand, I began working on building applications from the ground up, using the knowledge I gained from my previous experience. I downloaded the required software and started building the application. However, the company was more focused on merchandising and following up with suppliers for material procurement. This became my responsibility, and it was challenging to manage everything using an Excel file.

The journey to the company was 16 kilometers, about a 20-minute bike ride. Though it wasn't easy, there was beauty in that journey. The route was along the National Highway, with open spaces and small villages. During the winter, the scenery was breathtaking. I used to leave a little early to enjoy nature's beauty. The clear road, nearby mountains with clouds passing by, and the calmness of the villages gave me immense satisfaction in the morning.

When I returned during the rainy season, I enjoyed playing in the rain. Even if it rained after office hours, I didn't stop. Riding a bike in the rain has a different feeling. If you haven't tried it, you should.

I am thankful to our Creator for giving me the opportunity to work for this company. I learned a different job role and am proud of myself for putting my family first. I was jobless for 38 days and didn't let any opportunity pass. I agreed to this job with a lower salary because something is better than nothing. No experience or knowledge is ever wasted; it will prove useful in the future. The transition to a new role was daunting, but each day I felt a growing sense of accomplishment. The satisfaction of learning and adapting kept me motivated.

Now, you might wonder why I often express my gratitude to our Creator. Let me share a story about my ex-colleague, Mr. Rafi (May his soul rest in peace). He was a genuinely nice person, and we worked together in the same office. One day, he told me about a significant decision he made in his career.

Rafi had resigned from his job to pursue a higher salary. His boss, wanting to understand his decision, asked, "Rafi, what is your current salary?"

"6000 INR," Rafi replied.

His boss then explained, "Let's take an example of a person working in a Xerox shop earning the same salary. What are his responsibilities? He opens the shop, waits for customers, and if they come, he takes the xerox and doesn't gain any additional knowledge. Now, consider your job. You interact with customers and production teams, facing daily challenges. This experience can help you grow into a managerial role. That's why I always say, 'Salary is given by the owner, but the environment is given by our Creator.'"

His boss emphasized that this wasn't about belittling any job but recognizing that different roles offer different opportunities for growth and learning. These words of wisdom really struck me. At the time, my salary was less—an amount I could probably earn elsewhere without much trouble. But the unique experience and knowledge I was gaining in my current role were invaluable. Plus, I had the chance to enjoy the beauty of nature on my way to work every day.

This conversation made me realize that, while we might be tempted by higher salaries elsewhere, the environment and experiences we gain in our current roles are often more valuable in the long run. It's about recognizing the broader picture and appreciating the opportunities we have.

After a few months, I tried to implement features like production engineering for the manufacturing industry. The general manager and others focused more on productivity than system improvements. I adjusted my focus to align with theirs, which caused the development of applications to slow down.

Dealing with production people was a new experience. Their working nature differed from that of software developers. One supervisor blamed his production output on me, saying he hadn't received any input from me. I explained that he needed to provide target outputs, but he thought I worked under him. The conversation heated up, and in the middle of the production hall, I shouted that it wasn't my responsibility. The hall fell silent, and everyone was shocked by my outburst. The supervisor calmed down and followed my instructions.

I learned that we need to stand firm if we're right and apologize if we're wrong. Everyone has different levels of maturity and understanding.

I kept on searching for a new job because this one is temporary, as my main aim is to work for a Software Company, informing colleagues and relatives. After working for two more months, my distant relatives recommended the job in Chennai, 200 kilometers (about 124.27 miles) away. It was a metropolitan city with promising opportunities. The job was different from my previous role, as I was now offered a position as a store in-charge. The package was three times my current salary. I discussed it with my family, who were happy with the offer and advised me to go for the interview. This was one of the strangest interviews I've ever attended.

The interview was scheduled for 10 a.m. I left my hometown on a train at 5:30 a.m., reaching the city railway station on time. After a quick breakfast, I took a local bus to the company. The bus stopped nearby, and after asking for directions and walking for 10 minutes, I reached the company. It was beautifully maintained with lots of trees and plants, and the cleanliness was at the next level.

I informed security about the interview and called the interviewer, who asked me to wait in a meeting room as he had some urgent work to complete. I started dreaming about working there and enjoying the natural environment. One hour passed, then two hours, with no information about the interview. I thought it wouldn't be polite to call him, so I sent a reminder message. He replied, asking me to wait. By the third hour, I was bored. This was the first time I had to wait for someone this long.

Waiting is one of the toughest things in the world. You can spend hours with family, friends, or loved ones, but just sitting idle is tough. Nowadays, we have TikTok and YouTube shorts to pass the time, but back then, we didn't have such distractions.

As I sat waiting for hours, my initial excitement turned into anxiety. Each minute felt like an hour, and I questioned if this opportunity was slipping away. It was 1:30 in the afternoon, and I was hungry since I only had a light breakfast. I informed security that I would return after lunch. Just as I was leaving, I got a call to come back for the interview. It was like a little movie scene.

I hurried back, and as soon as I walked in, he said, "I'm sorry for the wait."

"It's okay," I replied, trying to hide my nervousness.

He asked about my experience, and I started explaining my role and what I had done so far. I also mentioned my expectations, especially considering the high living expenses in Chennai. He listened carefully and nodded.

"You have a good profile," he said, smiling. "I liked our interaction too. We actually have two openings: one here in Chennai and another in your hometown. Why not attend the other interview as well?"

I was a bit taken aback. "Really? That sounds interesting," I said, though a part of me wondered if this was just a polite way of suggesting I try elsewhere.

"Yes," he continued. "It's a good opportunity, and it might be more convenient for you."

I nodded, feeling a mix of hope and doubt. "Thank you. I'll definitely consider it."

I agreed, but inside I was a bit worried. Was this another way of saying no? I had faced many setbacks during interviews in the past.

He informed the other manager, gave his phone number, and asked me to go there immediately, as he would be there only for 1-2 hours.

I left the company. I called the second manager, who asked me to come before 3 PM. The distance between the two locations was almost 40 minutes by bus. I called my relative, who had proposed this job. He advised me to take the opportunity since I had traveled so far already, giving me a little boost.

I went to the second interview without having lunch. The manager arrived promptly, and we conducted the interview. He was looking for someone with good system knowledge, especially in Excel, and the ability to manage a warehouse and a team of 40+ employees. He was happy with my approach. My relative had advised me to ask for a higher salary, considering future increments might be slow.

When I stated my salary expectations, he accepted it at a high level and said that he was traveling abroad for work and would be back in two weeks. He promised to update me in 20 days. I wasn't sure if this was positive or negative. Usually, delays indicate a negative response.

I informed the first interviewer about this, and he advised me to wait for 20 days. My relative gave the same advice. I had my snacks for lunch and then returned home. I have already communicated this to my parents. They gave me hope over the phone and, even after my return, had positive hope that I would get this job. I continued with my current job. I kept track of the days on my calendar. On the 20th day, I called the manager, who said he had just returned and needed another 10 days. This made me think it wasn't worth pursuing further.

I started approaching other people for new job opportunities. On the 30th day, exactly as he said, I got a call from the manager saying they had agreed to the offer. Hearing this, I felt like I was flying with happiness. He asked me to start the job the next day.

There's a saying, "Sabar ka phal meetha hota hai," which means "The fruit of patience is sweet." I waited three hours for the first interview, traveled to the next one without lunch, and followed up patiently. Finally, the wait paid off.

As the manager expected me to join immediately, I hadn't mentioned I was working at another company. So, I didn't inform my current company and joined the new one the next day. This unprofessional step backfired.

The next day, I went to the new company, where my manager introduced me to the team and the current store in charge. He had resigned because he had a new opportunity in Nigeria. He was in his notice period and spent about two weeks handing over all the necessary tasks and knowledge to me.

There were around 40 workers, and a few staff members were also there. My role included managing these 40 employees, who were contract workers, and allocating their daily tasks. It was a new experience for me, and I found it rewarding. Additionally, I was responsible for regular weekly, daily, and monthly reporting to my manager. This wasn't just a store; it was an entire warehouse.

Since I joined the new company without informing my old company, they repeatedly called to know the status of the orders and why I wasn't coming to work. Initially, I didn't answer, but after multiple attempts, my old manager, who referred me for the job, called. He was also my friend, so I couldn't ignore his call. I explained everything to him.

"Why didn't you inform us?" he asked.

"I'm sorry," I replied. "I had to make a quick decision due to my situation."

He understood and was happy with my decision, but emphasized that leaving without notice was unprofessional.

"I knew it wasn't the right thing to do, but given my circumstances, I felt it was necessary," I said.

Later, I picked up the phone and called the owner of my old company. "Hello, sir. I need to inform you that I won't be returning," I said, bracing myself for his reaction.

He sounded angry at first. "Why didn't you tell us earlier? This is not professional," he said, his tone sharp.

I took a deep breath. "I understand, and I'm really sorry about that. I've been requesting a salary increase for months due to travel expenses, but my request wasn't granted. I had to make a quick decision for my family."

There was a moment of silence. Then he sighed. "I see. It's unfortunate, but given your situation, I understand. I accept your resignation."

"Thank you for understanding," I said, relieved. "I'll email all the pending tasks and order statuses right away."

Even today, I feel bad about how I left. It wasn't an easy decision, and the regret still lingers.

This decision reminds me of a man who once visited our home. He was a wise old man with lots of stories. My father, always curious, asked him, "Where do you live?"

The old man smiled and said, "If you ask anyone in my village, they will show you my house. Some will praise me, and some will scold me."

My father looked puzzled. "Why would anyone scold you if you haven't done anything wrong?"

The old man chuckled softly. "Even though I haven't done anything bad to anyone, my actions have indirectly affected them. You see, when we grow in our career or life, we make decisions that might benefit us but might not always please everyone around us. That's life."

This story stuck with me because it's true. As we progress, not everyone will be happy with our choices. It's part of the journey, and we must accept that we can't make everyone happy all the time.

I made this decision for my family, which impacted my former company. A quote that always resonates with me is, "Kuch paana hai to kuch khona hai"—if you need something, you need to lose something. From the company's perspective, what I did was not ethical, but from my perspective, it was the right call given the situation.

Leaving my old company without notice weighed heavily on me, but the responsibility of managing a large team kept me focused and driven. Managing employees requires a different skill set, especially when some are uneducated. I involved myself in their work and helped them, believing that just commanding wouldn't justify a leader's role. Working alongside them speeds up productivity. This approach had two benefits: employees felt their manager was working alongside them, which motivated them to work harder, and my tasks were completed more quickly.

One day, as I was helping to unload a shipment, one of the workers, Ramesh, came up to me. "Sir, it's really great to see you working with us," he said. "It makes us feel valued."

"Thank you, Ramesh," I replied, smiling. "We're all in this together. Your hard work is just as important as mine."

One evening, I discussed my new responsibilities with my parents. "It's challenging, but I'm learning a lot," I shared.

"We know you will achieve success in every field; we're proud of you," my mother replied. "Keep pushing forward."

This role taught me the value of delegation and teamwork. I learned that effective leadership involves working alongside your team and supporting them in their tasks. Thanks to our Creator, I had the opportunity to learn different skills at different stages of my life.

Interestingly, this was the same dream company where I had been rejected for a software role. I always thought I might get another chance to work in a software role here.

The previous owner wasn't interested in the application I developed, even though I worked on it late at night at home. I continued to build this application with my friend Niaz, who is now part of that project. Our application, DewDrops, focuses on the manufacturing sector.

Every change of job gives me a new role, which makes my journey interesting and challenging, and at the result is that I have gained knowledge and experience in various fields.

Hadith Inspiration:

"Allah will not be merciful to those who are not merciful to the people." (Sahih Bukhari)

Explanation: This Hadith emphasizes the importance of showing mercy and kindness to others. As I transitioned into a managerial role and dealt with various challenges, treating my team with kindness and understanding helped foster a positive working environment. It's a reminder that compassion in leadership brings about the best in people.

Motivational Quote:

"The best way to find yourself is to lose yourself in the service of others." — Mahatma Gandhi

Explanation: This quote encapsulates my experience of managing a large team and taking on new responsibilities. By focusing on serving my team and helping them succeed, I found greater fulfillment and purpose in my role. It highlights the importance of service and leadership in personal growth.

Questions for Reflection:

1. How do you handle situations where you feel overwhelmed by new responsibilities?
2. Have you ever felt pressured to perform well in a new job or role? How did you manage it?
3. What strategies do you use to stay calm and focused under pressure?
4. How do you balance learning new skills while managing your existing responsibilities?

Summary

In this chapter, I transitioned from a software role to a new job involving production, planning, and merchandising. I adapted to my new responsibilities, improving their Excel systems and starting new applications. The daily commute, though challenging, offered scenic beauty and peace.

I learned valuable lessons about different roles offering unique growth opportunities. Overcoming challenges in managing production, I balanced firmness with humility. Despite a lower salary, I accepted the job, knowing any experience is valuable.

A new opportunity in Chennai offered three times my current salary. The interview process was lengthy. Managing a team of 40 employees taught me the importance of teamwork and leadership. Despite initial regrets about leaving my previous job abruptly, I realized the necessity of balancing personal growth with family responsibilities. This chapter highlights the importance of adapting, continuous learning, and making tough decisions for a better future.

CHAPTER 6

TRANSITIONING TO SUCCESS

My life took a significant turn when I got married, which felt like a promotion in my personal life. I preferred an arranged marriage, trusting my parents' choice. While many people might not agree with this, I believed in their wisdom and judgment.

You might think I am a different person, not having any love stories in my life. Well, it's not like that. I do have a love story, just like everyone else. But since this book focuses on a different subject, I decided to keep my love story out of it.

If this book does well, then who knows? I may share that part of my life in a future book. There's always more to tell, and I look forward to sharing those stories with you too.

I took two weeks off from work for my marriage. After returning, my manager decided to give me a different role in procurement and planning. Being multi-skilled was beneficial, and I happily accepted the new responsibilities. This role allowed me to communicate with multiple people, clients, and suppliers, understand product making, and create production plans.

As I was completely involved in my regular office job, I still found time to work on developing the Dewdrop application with Niaz. We had a vision of selling our product and keeping it as a side hustle. Even with my busy schedule, I couldn't let go of my passion for software development. That's why I always say that working with software is in my veins. It's something I love and can't stop doing, no matter how packed my day is.

Day by day, I handled different kinds of challenges. After understanding the process, which took about two months, I consistently met my deliverables, while most of the other planners were struggling. Things were going smoothly until life took a sudden turn.

Whenever my life seems to be going smoothly, it takes a different direction.

We had a requirement from management to clear old stock items. I took a sample and showcased it to the client to get orders. The client agreed, but when it came time for the actual dispatch, the material did not match the sample due to the condition of the old stock. Some items had different colors. When I went to discuss this with the director, one of my colleagues advised me, "Be careful; the planning head is with the director. It might not be the best time."

"I need to explain the reality," I replied. I didn't listen to him and went to showcase the reality.

I explained the situation and returned to my work. I didn't know what the planning head informed the director. Later that evening, my assistant manager called me to his home and asked me about the issue. I was shocked and wondered why he suddenly called me.

"Why did you go to the director without waiting?" he asked.

"I needed to explain the situation," I replied.

He agreed and advised me that the planning head had already done similar things with other staff. He then informed me that the director had decided to suspend me for 10 days.

I was taken aback by this sudden turn of events. "Suspend me? For 10 days?" I asked, unable to conceal my shock.

"Yes," he said. "The director thinks it's the best course of action."

"This is office politics," I thought.

The news hit me hard. I couldn't believe that trying to be honest and transparent had backfired so badly. I had only wanted to explain the reality of the situation, but now I was being punished for it.

All of a sudden, my life took a reverse turn. I didn't know how to react. He tried to convince me that things would be normal after the suspension. It felt shameful. I came home and informed my parents. They were also shocked, and I decided to look for another job but not to resign immediately as it would impact my family. During the suspension, I spent quality time with my family, but internally, I was unsettled by the incident. If they had shouted at me for a mistake, warned me, or even fined me, it would have been okay. But suspending me for 10 days was not good.

I had done a lot of good work, saved money by converting old stock into usable products, and worked late nights to achieve targets. These things didn't matter to the company. That's why I remember the amazing quote by Dr. APJ Abdul Kalam:

"Love your job, but don't love your company, because you may not know when the company stops loving you." — Dr. APJ Abdul Kalam

When I returned after the suspension, the manager informed me that I would resume my old job as store in-charge, with no more planning work. Another setback was a kind of demotion. After this, I fixed my mind on looking for another job.

I started to look for another job and informed my friends about my decision. Despite doing my current job to support my family, I continuously worked on software during my free time or after office hours.

One of my school friends, Owes, called Niaz about an opportunity in Bangalore, which is about 200 km away from my hometown but in the opposite direction from Chennai. Niaz had been working there remotely for 1 or 2 months, but when they asked him to work from the Bangalore office, he refused due to his health issues. He informed me about the opportunity, and I inquired if I could take the job. The technology used in the project was new to me, particularly the front end. Niaz encouraged me to try it out and informed Owes, who then discussed it with the owner.

A few days later, Niaz, our friend Rafi, and I went on a local village trip on a Sunday evening. It was a relaxing day, and we were enjoying the change of scenery. Suddenly, Niaz received a call from Owes. He said that the owner wanted to discuss an opportunity with me.

The owner was a strong software networking person but didn't know much about application development. He relied on Owes for this. Owes asked me some basic questions about my experience and skills, and I agreed to take up the job. He believed I could quickly pick up the new technology.

"This is a new branch in Bangalore with a small office of five people, main head office is in Dubai" Owes explained. "It's not the big IT Company you might have hoped for, and the package is only slightly higher than your current salary. But the work is interesting, and there's a lot of potential for growth."

I thought about it for a moment. It wasn't the perfect opportunity, but it sounded promising. I agreed and asked for a 30-day notice period to wrap up my current job properly.

"The owner wants you to start after 20 days because of a client deadline," Owes said.

"Okay, I can manage that," I replied. "I'll start working from home for the first 10 days during my notice period. I'll work night hours to complete my notice period and support the new company."

So, I began balancing both jobs. It was challenging, but I was determined to make it work. This was a chance to step into something new and exciting, even if it wasn't exactly what I had envisioned.

I completed my notice period at the current company, leaving a good impression among the workers. Even today, after many years, when they meet me in the street, they are happy and wish I could be their in-charge. Hearing those words is so rewarding, knowing that I have made an impact on a few people's lives.

One of my mottos is "Make an Impact." We come into this world with a hidden life duration, but on average, people live around 60+ years. It's essential to make a positive impact during our time here.

Another important lesson I've learned is that we don't need a large circle of friends who add no real value to our lives. It's not about the quantity but the quality of the friendships that truly matters. Even if we have just a few friends, as long as they stand by us during our toughest times, they are a true blessing from our Creator. Such friends offer genuine support, understanding, and companionship when we need it the most, making them invaluable in our journey through life. Owes helped me with this job, but Niaz and Rafi are my closest friends and true gems in my life. I am lucky to have friends like them.

This job opportunity came through a call rather than a traditional IT interview. So far, all my interviews have been casual conversations, not highly technical ones. After this job, all my interviews became tech-specific as I stepped onto the proper IT ladder.

The upcoming chapters will explore a new and exciting journey filled with many achievements. Sometimes things do not go as planned, but our Creator is the best planner of all. I am truly grateful and thankful to my Creator.

One of the major turnarounds in my life was getting a job in Bangalore, the Silicon Valley of India. I thought that once I got there, I could switch jobs and settle down. But as they say, "We plan, and our Creator plans. Surely, our Creator is the best of planners."

I discussed the opportunity with my family. They were happy, especially my mother, who started dreaming of moving to Bangalore because of its beautiful weather. We hadn't made the decision to move yet because this was my first job outside my hometown. My wife was excited about the better package and the prospect of a good life, but she was initially concerned about being apart from me. Since Bangalore is 200 km away (almost a four-hour journey by road), I needed to stay in a PG (paying guest) and visit my hometown once a week.

I reached out to my friend Owes for directions and took my bike to the bus stand, then traveled by train to Bangalore. From the Bangalore railway station, I took a bus to the office, a journey of almost 5-6 hours. The office was located in a posh area with many small businesses. It wasn't in the IT hub, but the locality was fantastic.

"No worries; everything starts small to grow big." I accepted the job, and we went for a team lunch at a nearby restaurant. My boss, my friend, and Kartik—an amazing person who helped me a lot—were all there. Kartik had already found PGs for my stay and guided me around the area. We talked about our experiences.

"Kartik, how do you manage being away from your family?" I asked.

He smiled. "Everyone sacrifices something to achieve something. If you want to get something, you need to lose something."

This was an amazing sentence. I sacrificed time with my family for their better future, even though it was only for a short period.

I never had the experience of staying away from my family except on business visits to Germany for three weeks. In PG, we have multiple options. I stayed in a three-person room. There were 15 members in the PG. As an introvert, I initially found it difficult to adjust. My roommates were nice people from our neighboring state with great packages from big IT companies. They went home once every month or two, but I visited every week. I missed my family, wife, and friends. It's a common experience when we detach from our usual environment and live in a new place.

Two months passed, and I felt hopeful about the company's future. I discussed with my family and finalized the decision to move to Bangalore.

Quranic Inspiration:

"And We will surely test you with something of fear and hunger and a loss of wealth and lives and fruits, but give good tidings to the patient." - Surah Al-Baqarah (2:155)

Explanation: This verse perfectly captures the essence of this period. My faith in our Creator's plan helped me remain patient and resilient through the trials of adapting to a new city and managing financial strains.

Motivational Quote:

"Success is not the key to happiness. Happiness is the key to success. If you love what you are doing, you will be successful." – Albert Schweitzer

Explanation: This quote resonates deeply with my journey. Finding happiness in my new roles and embracing the changes with a positive mindset was essential. My love for my work and the support of my family helped me navigate the challenges and find success in a new environment.

Questions for Reflection:

1. Have you ever made a significant career change? What motivated your decision?
2. How do you weigh the pros and cons when making a major life decision?
3. What role does faith play in your decision-making process?
4. How do you cope with the uncertainty that comes with taking a leap of faith?

Summary

In this chapter, my life took a significant turn with marriage, which felt like a promotion in my personal life. Trusting my parents' choice for an arranged marriage and returning to work, I was given a new role in procurement and planning, expanding my skills. Despite my busy schedule, I continued developing the Dewdrop application with Niaz, maintaining my passion for software.

Challenges at work arose, including a disheartening 10-day suspension due to office politics. Determined to move forward, I found a promising job in Bangalore through my friend Owes. The new role offered potential growth, even though it required me to stay away from my family initially.

Balancing both jobs was tough, but I completed my notice period professionally and started the new job, which involved managing a warehouse and a team. This experience taught me the value of quality friendships and making a positive impact. Ultimately, my family and I decided to move to Bangalore for a better future.

PART 4

RESILLIENCE AND ACHIEVEMENTS

CHAPTER 7

AN I.T JOB WITH UNEXPECTED TWISTS

We lived in a rented house with my parents, my brother's family, and my own. Each month, my brother and I would give a certain amount to my mother to help manage the household expenses. This is a very good method for managing the family.

I've seen many families where, as their kids grow up and start earning, the parents assign specific responsibilities to each child. For instance, Kid1 might be in charge of the electricity and water bills, while Kid2 handles groceries, vegetables, and fruits. However, this approach has its drawbacks. It can lead to imbalances and misunderstandings if one child's responsibilities are more financially demanding or time-consuming than the others. It might also create a sense of division rather than unity.

In my opinion, parents should continue collecting a monthly contribution from each child to manage household expenses, as they did before. This method ensures efficient handling of the family's finances are maintains a sense of unity and shared responsibility. It avoids potential conflicts and keeps the family functioning as a cohesive unit, just like in the earlier days.

We all gathered to discuss the opportunity and the situation at hand. It wasn't an easy decision, as it involved significant changes for everyone. After carefully considering all the factors, including our financial situation, work opportunities, and family dynamics, we finally concluded that the best course of action was for my brother to shift to his in-laws' house. This move would give us the flexibility and space we needed to transition smoothly.

My brother's move to his in-laws' house meant he would have a stable living arrangement while we moved to Bangalore. This decision ensured that my brother was well taken care of, allowing us to focus on the new opportunities in Bangalore without worrying about arrangements back home.

It was a collective decision, reflecting our family's ability to come together and support each other during times of change.

This decision wasn't just about logistics; it was also about emotional and practical support. My brother's in-laws welcomed him, understanding the circumstances and offering their support. This made it easier for us to accept the decision, knowing he was in good hands. Meanwhile, we prepared for our move to Bangalore, packing up our belongings and making arrangements for our new life.

The move to Bangalore marked a new chapter in our lives. It was filled with excitement and a bit of anxiety as we ventured into an unfamiliar city. However, knowing that my brother was well settled gave us peace of mind. The process of finding a new home, adapting to a new environment, and starting afresh in Bangalore was made smoother by our collective decision-making and the support of our extended family.

In the end, our family's strength and unity shone through. The move demonstrated our ability to adapt, support each other, and make decisions that benefited everyone. It was a testament to our resilience and the strong bond that held us together, enabling us to face new challenges with confidence and optimism.

I usually consider various perspectives in every situation. I like to take a step back and understand the situation from different perspectives before making any decisions. So, when this opportunity in Bangalore came up, I did just that.

I sat down with my wife and had a heart-to-heart conversation. "Look," I said, "if everything goes well, we can settle down in Bangalore. It's a big move, but it could be great for us." She nodded, understanding the excitement and the apprehension. "But if things don't work out as planned," I continued, "we'll reassess our situation before our kids start school. We have a bit of time to figure things out since our first child is less than a year old right now. We're looking at a 3-4 year window to make this decision."

Having this conversation with my wife was important. We both needed to be on the same page and prepared for any outcome. It wasn't just about the move; it was about making sure our family's future was secure and that we were making the best decision for our children's upbringing.

"Let's give it a shot," my wife said with a reassuring smile. "We can handle whatever comes our way." Her confidence gave me the boost I needed. Knowing that we had some time to reassess things if needed made the decision feel less daunting. It was comforting to know we had a few years to settle in and decide if Bangalore was the right place for us.

During this two-month period, our company expanded a bit and hired three people for marketing. One colleague, Imthiyaz, was from Hyderabad but had relatives in Bangalore. He helped me search for a home. We found a place with a first and second floor—he took the first floor, and I took the second.

Nowadays, people often prefer nuclear families. It's a shift from the traditional joint family setup, and both types have their own pros and cons. On one hand, a nuclear family provides privacy and freedom. You have your own space to make decisions without the constant input of extended family members. It allows you to run your household exactly the way you want, which can be liberating.

But on the other hand, a nuclear family lacks the daily support of an extended family. In a joint family, there's a constant presence of love and support. It's like having a mini-celebration every day. You share responsibilities, which makes life a bit easier. Tasks like cooking, cleaning, and looking after children are divided, and there's always someone to lend a hand or offer advice. The house is filled with laughter, stories, and a sense of togetherness that makes every day special.

Despite the convenience of nuclear families, the warmth and camaraderie of joint families are irreplaceable. Nowadays, people use smartphones and video calls to stay connected with their loved ones remotely. While technology helps bridge the gap, it can't replace the emotional bond of being physically present. The hug of a grandparent, the shared meal around a large dining table, the spontaneous conversations that happen when everyone is under one roof—these are the moments that technology can't replicate.

Some families choose to live apart due to personal preferences, seeking the independence that a nuclear family offers. Others are separated by circumstances such as job opportunities in different cities or countries. Whatever the reason, the shift to nuclear families often comes with a mix of excitement and longing.

I took this decision due to our situation. My brother wasn't willing to move to Bangalore because his expertise was more valued in our hometown.

"I understand why we need to move," my wife said. "But it's hard to leave everyone behind."

"I know," I replied, "but we have to do what's best for our future." I controlled my emotions in front of my family.

We booked a transport and reached Bangalore around 1 AM. We unloaded everything and took 1-2 days to settle down. My entire family came to help set things up. This is one of the beauties of being in a joint family.

As mentioned in the Hadith, there is benefit for taking cumulative decisions. Sometimes, we need to make decisions that impact others' lives. In such situations, it's crucial to discuss with all stakeholders. This helps avoid misunderstandings and maintain healthy relationships. In my case, despite the impact on my brother, we maintain the same bond because we made a joint decision.

We were all thrilled to be living in a dream city and working in a software company. It felt like a new chapter full of excitement and opportunities. My colleague and neighbor, Imtiyaz, played a big role in helping me settle into this new life. He was like a guide, showing me around the city and helping me discover all the hidden gems, especially the food spots.

Every day, we would commute together on a single bike. Depending on the traffic, the ride would take anywhere from 20 to 40 minutes. It was during these rides that we bonded the most. On the way back home, we often made it a point to stop and try different snacks at various places. Street vendors, small cafes, or famous food joints—we explored them all. Thanks to Imtiyaz, I got to know so many amazing places in the city that I wouldn't have found on my own.

As the month passed, I realized I had spent my entire salary, ending the month with a zero balance. I was concerned about managing the family and saving for the future, as the cost of living was higher than I had anticipated. Back home, I used to give 10k from my salary, and with my brother's contribution, my mother managed the household smoothly, even purchasing appliances on EMI.

With 40k in Bangalore, I struggled to manage my monthly expenses. I usually take pre-calculated risks, but due to a lack of experience, I underestimated some costs. At the month's end, my bank balance was zero.

"Why didn't you warn me about these extra expenses?" I complained to my parents.

"We thought you knew," they replied. "You've always managed well before." Though my expenses were within my salary, the constant worry about making ends meet kept me up at night. I questioned if moving to Bangalore was the right decision.

As the saying goes, "Necessity is the mother of invention." Coming from a lower-middle-class family, I was eager to earn more money. One of my colleagues, Hussain, and I discussed part-time job opportunities. My hometown is famous for Ambur Biryani and leather footwear. He suggested starting a footwear business in Bangalore. We decided to buy some samples and try selling them.

We started a company, printed visiting cards, and invested 5k each to buy shoes. I went to my hometown, purchased some shoes, and tried to sell them both online and offline. The offline market was tough, but we sold all the shoes online and shared the profit equally.

Next, I bought shoes on credit for 30k from my friends in the footwear trading business. I found a garment store nearby that liked the product and purchased the entire quantity. I returned the money to my friends within three days.

This success made me realize the potential of the business.

"Hussain, I think we need a bigger investment to grow this business," I said.

"I understand," he replied. "But I need some time to arrange. I can't invest more right now."

I decided to part ways with Hussain, as I needed a larger investment to grow. I continued selling shoes online and at nearby shops, earning a substantial amount.

Even today, I feel bad about my decision to part ways with Hussain. To make up for it, I motivated and guided him in the best possible ways to expand his finance consulting business, which he did successfully, earning a lot.

I got an opportunity to work for a Dubai-based company and, by God's grace, also visit Dubai for an official project. Last time, I went to Germany for a business trip, and this time to Dubai, which seemed amazing. I went there for three weeks. Thanks to the owner (Mr. Mahaboob Basha).

Before visiting Dubai, while I was still running my side footwear business, I had some inventory left at my home. I decided to give it to one of my regular customers who owns a shop near my home in Bangalore. I had done good business with them before. I explained to him that I was going to Dubai for office work, handed over the stock, and asked him to pay me within a week. He agreed.

That was my last business transaction. Since then, I have only received 20% of the amount. Despite multiple attempts and various methods, I have yet to receive the remaining balance. Doing business is a skill, and I took a calculated risk, which resulted in a loss in my profit, though not in my principal amount. As you read on, you will understand the reasons why I decided to stop the business.

It was a learning experience for me in Dubai, as I had to stay in a labor camp. Nowadays, these areas have beautiful apartment-like setups where people working for different companies can stay peacefully. Rooms are shared by 4-8 members, but as a visitor, I got a separate room.

The client was one of the largest groups in the construction domain. They were very kind and explained the entire process of how they manage employees on construction sites, every detail of it. This helped me build the logic in the application and its reports.

My ex-colleague Akbar, whom I mentioned earlier about my Dubai job getting canceled and me being jobless for 38 days, is now working in Dubai and living in Sharjah. We are still friends, he was happy about my visit and invited me to his home for a delicious dinner.

During the weekend, he picked me up from my room, and we roamed in and around Dubai and its nearby places in his car. We went to a nearby beach, which was peaceful, neat, and clean. The major highlight was the Ras-Al-Khaimah Mountains. On the way, we stopped at a mosque for prayer, and when we returned, fresh dates from a nearby tree were waiting for us. We picked a few and tasted them; they tasted great, were fresh, and were fully ripened from the tree. Even though my hometown was surrounded by mountains, these mountains were five times taller. I was amazed and terrified by the route and location. After reaching the top of the mountain, I saw many locals preparing Barbeque dishes for their dinner. I asked Akbar about it, and he said it was regular for locals during weekends to come out with family and enjoy dinner outside.

The next weekend, I called my cousin Huresh, who was working there. He guided me on the bus and metro routes to reach a place where he also came from. We roamed around within Dubai city, visiting Burj Khalifa, Burj Al Arab, and its beach beside it—all were amazing and pleasing to my eyes. We were tired, and he directed me to the correct bus for reaching my destination. I made the same mistake I did during my first job—I got off at the first bus stop. Either I had to wait 15 minutes for another bus or take a cab, which was four times more expensive than the bus. It was already 9 PM, so instead of waiting, I picked up a cab and informed the driver of my location. Due to his urgency, he dropped me off at another location where he needed to park his car. I argued with him, but he didn't apologize and went away.

I had a smartphone with me, and when I looked for the location, it said it was 2 km away on a highway with no shops around, and the nearest bus stop was half a kilometer away. I blamed myself for this mistake; it would have been better to wait for a few more minutes for a regular bus. With no other choice, I started walking towards the bus stop. After walking for a while, I saw a bus pass by. I signaled the driver to stop, and he did after a short distance due to the speed of the bus. I ran to the bus and sat down, realizing that it was actually my destination. From there, I walked to my room, thanked God, and slept.

One valuable lesson I learned is to avoid taking shortcuts or rushing through things. It's important to stay calm and patient. Everything will happen in its own time.

I love to travel and see the beautiful creations of our Creator. The earth we live on is here for us. Our Creator has made it for us, so we should travel as much as possible within our capabilities. Every region and every part of the world has a different culture. Traveling allows us to understand different cultures and the behaviors of various kinds of people.

The company's situation wasn't good; there were no clients. I attended a few interviews but failed due to a lack of knowledge. I still remember one interview where I tried to give the answers, but the interviewer didn't seem happy. I told him, "I'm a practical guy. I don't know all the technical phrases, but if you ask me practical questions, I can answer." He agreed, took out a piece of paper, and began asking me a few questions. I gave some answers, but there were many I didn't know. After that, he seemed sad and said, "Out of 10, I can't even give you 0.5. Maybe you are doing a good job in your present company, but based on your answers, this is my judgment."

That struck me very hard. Two things I realized: One, I needed to learn things from the basics and practice a lot to understand the concepts in depth. Two, working in a small company or on small projects doesn't give us the difficult challenges we get in bigger organizations. This experience opened my eyes. I started looking for things that could spark my interest and give me the opportunity to learn and grow.

I explored Tableau, a data analytics tool, but it wasn't free. Then I discovered Power BI, which was free, and it has changed my life. I'll cover more about this in a future chapter.

Feeling disheartened but determined, I decided to return home for my child's education and our future. Sometimes, life throws challenges at us to push us towards growth. It reminded me of the words of Albert Einstein: "In the middle of difficulty lies opportunity."

This experience taught me the importance of constant learning and seeking out challenges that help us grow. It wasn't easy, but it was necessary for my personal and professional development.

Another pivotal time in my life has arrived. When I moved to Bangalore, we had 3-4 years to settle into a well-established company for a bright future. If I didn't get that opportunity, I would return to my hometown. I thought the small company I joined would grow soon. They started with three people and expanded to seven. However, due to fewer projects, they had to close. Despite this, my boss managed to pay my salary on time. Over the past few months, I have been the only person working on maintaining the project application. Eventually, the company closed.

I lost hope of getting a job in Bangalore and decided to return home. By God's grace, I heard of an opportunity in my hometown at the dream company I was previously rejected from. They couldn't match my Bangalore salary but offered 70% of it.

"We can manage with a lower salary here," my wife said. "The cost of living is less, and we'll be closer to family."

"I agree," I replied. "Let's take this opportunity."

I searched for a rental home near a school, grocery store, and mosque for my father. I also planned to do a part-time job with friends in the footwear business. We found a suitable house and moved from Bangalore to our hometown. The new company was about three kilometers from home. Everything settled well. I enrolled my son in a nearby school.

Hadith Inspiration:

"The best of you are those who are best to their families." (Sunan al-Tirmidhi)

Explanation: This Hadith underscores the importance of being good to our families. Throughout my struggles and ventures, ensuring the well-being of my family was my top priority. It's a reminder that our first responsibility is towards our family, and kindness towards them is highly valued.

Motivational Quote:

"It is not the strongest of the species that survive, nor the most intelligent, but the one most responsive to change." — Charles Darwin

Explanation: This quote highlights the importance of adaptability. My journey through family transitions, financial struggles, and business ventures required me to adapt continuously. It's a reminder that flexibility and responsiveness to change are crucial for survival and success.

Questions for Reflection:

1. How do you stay positive and proactive during periods of unemployment or financial difficulty?
2. What steps do you take to seek new opportunities when faced with joblessness?
3. How do you balance your personal goals with your family's needs and expectations?
4. How do you maintain your self-esteem and motivation during challenging times?

Summary

Living in a joint family, my brother and I contributed to household expenses. To streamline finances, we decided my brother would move to his in-laws' house, allowing us to transition smoothly to Bangalore. This decision ensured that everyone was well taken care of and demonstrated our family's unity.

In Bangalore, adjusting to the new environment was both exciting and challenging. My colleague, Imtiyaz, helped us settle in.

Financial challenges soon surfaced, and I struggled with the higher cost of living. Partnering with a colleague, I started a small footwear business to supplement my income. I faced career setbacks, including failed interviews and company closures, which prompted my return home.

Returning to my hometown brought stability.

This journey underscored the importance of resilience, adaptability, and continuous learning in overcoming life's unexpected twists.

CHAPTER 8

A LEAP OF FAITH

We were four friends: Rafi, Niaz, Tabrez, and I. We started a footwear business unit called TRAN—T for Tabrez, R for Rafi, A for Adnan, and N for Niaz. During that time, they wanted us to invest in starting the business. Niaz and Rafi each started with a capital of 50K INR. I couldn't invest because my marriage was nearby, and I needed to take care of those expenses.

They made good progress. During my free time, I helped them with their process. A few months later, they planned to expand and asked for more investment. By this time, my wife was pregnant, and I needed to take care of hospital and post-delivery expenses, so I didn't invest even the second time.

"Niaz, I'm sorry, but I can't invest right now," I said.

"I understand," he replied. "Family comes first."

Now, they have grown much bigger and are doing great business. I wish them continued success. The main partners are Rafi and Niaz. Tabrez also didn't invest due to his family situation. Watching Rafi and Niaz succeed made me question my decisions. Did I make the right choice by prioritizing my marriage over the investment? Marriage is one of the most beautiful gifts from our Creator. If we get the right partner, then our life will be like heaven on earth. I convinced myself that I had made the right decision.

The point I want to highlight is that opportunities don't come often. Some say we need to create opportunities, while others believe they come all the time. In reality, opportunities are rare. If we strike while the iron is hot, we can make a significant difference.

Every time I've faced a major decision, it comes with two options. For instance, I had to choose between investing in the business and covering my marriage expenses. To me, completing my marriage was the most important thing. I decided to use the funds for my wedding rather than investing.

I also realized that people change as they grow. This book's concept revolves around this idea. We grow up in our parents' environment, whether in a single or joint family. Our upbringing shapes the qualities we develop. As we grow, we interact with friends from different backgrounds, influencing our skills and behaviors.

"In school, we may pick up good or bad habits," my father said. "Some parents manage to guide their children back on track, while others struggle. The next stage is college, where we further develop behaviors influenced by friends and the environment."

College is a new world, my father said. "Stay focused and choose your friends wisely."

After college comes the stage of starting a job or business. Our behavior is shaped by our background and the people we encounter. Then comes marriage, where partners influence each other based on their experiences. Finally, having kids adds responsibility, impacting our thinking and priorities. It's our duty to provide proper parenting and fulfill our children's needs.

I hoped to work for a company in my hometown while also taking a part-time job with my friends' business. However, they had grown significantly, employing many people, and there was no scope for me to join them.

I needed to find a way to support my family because my salary was only sufficient to manage our daily expenses. I wanted a brighter future, a dream house, a good education for my kids, and the ability to travel, one of my passions. So, I started looking for other options.

I searched the Internet for ways to earn a side income. I found an article describing 15 ways to generate passive income. Two things stood out to me: writing a book and creating content on YouTube.

"Which one should I choose?" I asked my wife. "Writing a book or starting a YouTube channel?"

"You love Power BI," she said. "Why not start with that on YouTube?"

I was good with Microsoft Power BI, a Data Analytics tool that changed my life. People say every successful person has a supportive woman behind them. I agree. First, my mom, and then my wife. I also credit Power BI for transforming my career. I am grateful to those who developed Power BI and Microsoft for providing this tool.

I wondered which option to pursue. Writing a book seemed daunting because I didn't think I had any stories to tell. At that time, I felt I had no significant achievements to motivate readers. But now, reflecting on my life, I realize I've faced many challenges worth sharing. That's why I started writing this book.

Back then, I decided to create content on YouTube (Channel name: taik18). I started in my bedroom, recording audio-only content about Power BI. Only my wife knew about this. I recorded while my kids and parents slept because I didn't want them to know about my side gig. I wanted to save this money for our future.

Creating content required a lot of effort. I had to learn new skills, research, develop content, record, edit, publish, and share. It took 5-7 hours to produce a 15-minute video. Content creation is different from professional work, with a separate learning curve. Since then, I've been regularly making

YouTube videos. Initially, I only had 4 or 5 views, but I was happy. My goal wasn't short-term success, but long-term impact. I aimed to create a channel that would provide stable income after a few years and continue during my retirement.

During the lockdown, many people started their own YouTube channels on Power BI and other topics. Some of them grew rapidly, surpassing mine. I don't know the exact reason behind the YouTube algorithm, but I continue to produce content, believing it's a long-term journey.

During that period, YouTube recommended some videos to me. I was curious to see what these guys were talking about, especially Ankur Warikoo and Pranjal Kamra. They are truly great and provide valuable insights on personal finance. Their videos gave me direction in life, teaching me how to manage finances, tackle difficult situations, balance current wishes with future goals, and prioritize things like term insurance, emergency funds, and health insurance.

At this time, I was working in an IT company (I have covered the topic of how I landed in an IT company in the next chapter), and by God's grace, finances weren't a problem. Managing them properly was the challenge. After watching many videos, I learned about the stock market and Fixed Deposits (FD).

Fixed Deposits (FD) is the safest investment one can start and invest in, but this is not allowed in Islam due to interest from the bank, so I didn't start this.

Regarding the stock market, I knew about it before but thought it was a scam. The more I researched, the more interested I became. However, trading full-time requires a deep understanding of business balance sheets, profit and loss statements, performance trends, and global market movements. I couldn't commit to being a full-time trader.

Further research led me to mutual funds, which don't require full-time attention. By investing regularly each month, fund managers handle the rest for a reasonable fee. In Islam, there are many restrictions on where we can invest. Businesses involved in alcohol, pork products, or interest-based finance are not permissible. These are called Sharia-compliant stocks. Out of 4000 companies listed on the stock market, nearly 1000 are compliant. For mutual funds, only 2 or 3 were available at that time. I began investing through a Systematic Investment Plan (SIP), which I continue to do for my retirement.

As I worked with Power BI, I regularly checked the community for questions and tried to answer as many as possible. If a question particularly interested me, I would make a video for my channel. I also shared my knowledge through online conferences.

After significant community involvement from home during the pandemic, I decided to pursue the MVP (Microsoft Valuable Professional) award, given by Microsoft for impactful community contributions to various technical tools. With my YouTube videos over the past three years and speaking engagements at online conferences, I met the criteria. I approached David Abu, an MVP from Nigeria, through Twitter, and he kindly helped me with the nomination process. After submitting the required documents and completing the verification process, I was awarded the MVP title.

Receiving this award was an incredibly joyful moment. The first thought that crossed my mind was how happy my mom would have been to see this. I was the first person in my hometown to receive this award, and at that time, only 42 MVPs existed in my entire state in the Data Platform category. It was a great honor to be recognized by Microsoft for my contributions to the community. I am deeply thankful to our Creator for this achievement.

Quranic Inspiration:

"And whatever good you put forward for yourselves – you will find it with Allah. It is better and greater in reward." (Quran 73:20)

Explanation: This verse emphasizes that any good we do for ourselves will be rewarded by Allah. Pursuing new opportunities, building a YouTube channel, and managing personal finances were steps towards bettering myself and my family's future. It's a reminder that our efforts, especially in seeking good, are valued and rewarded by Allah.

Motivational Quote:

"The road to success and the road to failure are almost exactly the same." – Colin R. Davis

Explanation: This quote captures the essence of my journey. Both paths are filled with challenges, but the difference lies in persistence and learning from failures. My passion for Power BI and my commitment to helping others through my content brought me immense joy. This happiness fueled my success, leading to recognition from Microsoft. The MVP Award was not just a testament to my skills but also a validation of my dedication to making a positive impact on the community.

Questions for Reflection:

1. How do you handle major life changes, such as moving to a new city or changing jobs?
2. What strategies do you use to adapt to new environments and situations?
3. How do you support your family during times of transition and uncertainty?
4. What lessons have you learned from embracing change in your life?

Summary

I started a footwear business with my friends, Rafi, Niaz, and Tabrez, called TRAN. Due to personal expenses, I couldn't invest, but I helped them during my free time. Despite feeling left out as they grew, I believed prioritizing my family was the right decision.

Opportunities don't come often, and making choices isn't easy. Reflecting on life's stages—from school, college, and work to marriage and parenthood—I realized how these experiences shape us. As my friends' business flourished, I sought ways to support my family. I sought passive income ideas online and decided to create YouTube content about Power BI, recording videos discreetly at night.

I learned a lot about finance from influencers like Ankur Warikoo and Pranjal Kamra, which helped me manage my finances better. My dedication to Power BI led me to community involvement, ultimately earning me the prestigious MVP (Microsoft Valuable Professional) award. This recognition was a proud moment, reminding me of my journey and the importance of perseverance and family support.

CHAPTER 9

FINDING GROWTH IN UNEXPECTED PLACES

One of the saddest moments of my life was when my mother passed away. She was my backbone, and it happened so suddenly. One day, she experienced upper back pain, which she sometimes had due to gastric issues. She took some medicine and went to sleep. The next morning, around 7:00 AM, the pain started again. Believing it was due to the gastric issue, we rushed her to the hospital. They gave her some medicine, and she felt a little better. I then went to the office.

Later that day, around noon, I got a call from my father saying my mom still wasn't feeling well. They decided to visit another doctor, specifically our family doctor. He asked them to rush to the hospital because his clinic didn't have the necessary facilities. My father called me, and I immediately returned from work. We sought other doctors' opinions; my manager's wife is also a doctor. I shared the report with them, and they also suggested going to a bigger hospital.

We booked a cab and went there. During the transit, I asked my mom how she was feeling. She said she had a bit of chest pain, but nothing major. When we reached the hospital, she walked to the emergency ward herself and explained her condition to the doctors. They started checking her and asked me to handle the admissions process and payment. While I was in line, I got a call from my sister saying my mom was not responding. I rushed back to find the doctors performing CPR. I saw the ECG monitor showing a flat line. I spoke loudly, hoping my mom could hear me. "Don't worry, I'm here. All will be okay." I saw a little movement on the monitor, but it soon went flat again. That was it.

The doctors tried everything, but she didn't make it. It all happened within a single day. She had never been a burden to anyone. That's the beauty of our Creator. We don't know when we'll arrive in this world, and we don't know when we'll leave. We need to be humble, responsible, and impactful with our time so that others can benefit from it.

My mother's life had a profound impact on me and our relatives. She raised us to be well-behaved and educated, even if we weren't highly qualified. The qualities she instilled in us make her an inspirational person.

"I don't know how we'll manage without her," I confided to my wife.

"We'll take it one day at a time," she replied, holding my hand.

After her passing, the place where we lived brought back too many memories of her. It created a sad environment, so I decided to move to a new home. Living in a rented house made it easy to relocate. I believed that changing our environment would help us move on with life.

I now had a bigger responsibility. I had been managing family expenses for the last 2-3 years with my mother's help. If I needed advice, she was always there. Now, the entire responsibility was on me. I needed to take care of my father, wife, and kids.

We looked for a new house and found an apartment. We had negative experiences with houses where the owner lived in the same building. My father suggested finding a place where all families were tenants. We found an apartment near a good school, a mosque, and grocery stores. Even though it was smaller and the rent was 50% higher,

My brother and I decided to talk to the owner about either increasing the advance amount or reducing the rent. We approached him and asked, "Could you possibly increase the advance amount or lower the monthly rent for us?"

The owner, who has many rental properties, responded firmly, "I don't need any extra rent; I need a steady monthly income. The rent is fixed. If you want to take the place, that's fine, if not, that's perfectly acceptable as well."

Then he shared a bit of his own story. "You know," he began, "I faced a lot of struggles while building this apartment. There's an old saying: 'Shaadi karko dekh, Ghar banko dekh.' It means, 'Do a marriage, build a house,' and it highlights that you will face many struggles until it's complete."

We listened, understanding that he was trying to convey how challenging it can be to achieve these big milestones in life. We decided to move for the betterment of our family. It was one of the best decisions I've made.

I always consider every angle before making a decision because narrow thinking can lead to future troubles. The school near the new apartment was one of the best in town, and the location was convenient for everything we needed.

After moving, our family environment slowly started to change. As days passed, things began to return to normal.

One of the biggest issues we faced was the COVID-19 pandemic. It changed many lives, some for the better and some for the worse. If you're not aware, COVID-19 is a disease that spreads rapidly through the air. If it is not treated early, it can be fatal. Millions of people were affected globally. Similar situations have occurred in the past, almost 100 years ago.

The COVID-19 pandemic negatively impacted most industries, except for the pharma, hospital, and IT sectors, which experienced a boom. Unfortunately, the manufacturing company I worked for was severely affected. They reduced salaries by 20-30%, making it difficult for me to manage regular family expenses. I withdrew my PF balance to support my family during these difficult times.

I discussed the situation with my wife. The salary cut was a heavy blow. I could see the worry in my wife's eyes, and it pained me to think about the future we had envisioned for our children.

"What are we going to do now?" my wife asked, her voice tinged with concern.

"We'll find a way," I assured her. "I'll start looking for other opportunities."

I needed to earn more. I believed that our Creator would help us. Although it is said that what is destined for you will come to you, I knew that I needed to work towards my goals. Let me share a story to illustrate this point.

There were two friends, PA and PB. PA said, "I'll sit on top of a tree, and our Creator will give me something to eat." PB replied, "That's not right. You need to work for your food. Then you can earn money and buy food." PA disagreed and insisted that the Creator would provide for him. So, he climbed a tree and waited. Hours passed, and nobody noticed him. Eventually, a family came to eat lunch under the tree. PA thought they would notice him and give him food, but they didn't. Desperate, he coughed to get their attention. They saw him and offered food, and PA came down to eat.

PA later told PB, "You said the Creator wouldn't provide food without work, but I got food." PB asked for the full story and said, "The cough was the work you did to get their attention. You still had to put in an effort to receive the food. Similarly, in life, we need to do something to achieve our goals. We can't just sit idle and expect things to happen."

In the COVID situation, starting a business was not a viable solution. Starting a part-time job was also not an option due to lockdowns and restrictions. Many people started new businesses or part-time jobs during this period because companies laid off employees and they needed to find alternative income sources. The healthcare and IT sectors thrived as they adapted to the new normal and embraced innovative approaches.

As I continued to make YouTube videos on Power BI and work at my company, I realized I had developed a deep knowledge of the software. This made it easier for me to attend interviews and confidently answer questions. I updated my resume and applied for jobs through job portals. I received a call from a consulting company, attended the interview, and got the job with a 250% salary hike from my current pay, which was almost a 400% hike compared to the reduced salary during the pandemic.

I gave my resignation, and though they were reluctant to let me go, they couldn't match the new salary. Eventually, they agreed, and I served the notice period. After that, I joined the software company.

This was one of the proudest moments of my life. From the very beginning, I had been hoping and striving to get a job in the IT sector. After almost 15 years of hard work, persistence, and unwavering determination, I finally achieved my dream.

This journey taught me a valuable lesson: never give up on your dreams, no matter how long it takes or how many obstacles you face. Each challenge is an opportunity to grow stronger and more resilient. As the saying goes, "The harder the struggle, the more glorious the triumph" — Thomas Paine.

My experience reminds us all that perseverance and faith can lead to incredible achievements. If you keep pushing forward and believe in yourself, you can overcome any hurdle and reach your goals. Keep moving forward, stay dedicated, and remember that every step, no matter how small, brings you closer to your dream.

This experience reminded me of a frog that first pushes itself backward before making a big leap forward. Just like the frog, sometimes we need to stop for a moment, look closely at our situation, and get ready before taking a big step. This pause helps us gather the strength and clarity we need to move ahead successfully.

After working with a good salary in the IT sector for a few years, like everyone else, my biggest dream was to buy a home. My mother's greatest wish was to have a house of our own. Since my childhood, even though we lived in my grandfather's house for a while, we eventually moved to a rented house when I was in the 6th standard. Since then, we have been living in rented accommodations. Despite the challenges, my mother managed to run the family smoothly without much struggle for us. However, I witnessed the difficulties my family faced during my childhood until I started earning. This made me realize the value of money. No matter your degree, position, or status, without money, there is little respect in society.

So, I saved diligently by working multiple jobs simultaneously, a practice known as moonlighting. My Initial plan was to use my income to buy land and build a house without taking any loans, as interest is prohibited in Islam and can be a burden until fully repaid.

I called several agents and searched for over 100 flats and houses for almost a year, but couldn't find anything within my budget in our hometown. Finally, I found a flat in a local area I liked. There are many things to check before buying land to avoid issues like duplicate documents, unapproved land, or properties sold to multiple people. I bought the flat, gave the advance, and prepared for registration. However, the actual owners were different from the sellers, and the main documents were missing. Despite waiting and repeated arguments, I eventually got my money back with the help of my father-in-law, brother-in-law, and others.

A similar situation happened to one of my friends. He bought a piece of land from someone, and just a few days after he started building his house, another person showed up and told him to stop because the property actually belonged to him. Confused, my friend checked the documents and other details, and it turned out that this other person had also bought the same land. It was a trick; somehow, they had managed to sell one property to two people.

My friend was devastated. He filed lots of complaints with the relevant authorities, hoping to sort things out. But after a lot of back and forth, he eventually lost hope. In the end, he had to let go of the property entirely. We need to check all the related documents and verify them before purchasing any property.

I resumed my search and found another house that my wife and I both liked. We decided to purchase it, feeling a sense of excitement and joy at the prospect of finally owning our dream home. However, this time, there was a shortage of funds. I had a property to sell, but it didn't sell due to its location and size. Determined to make our dream a reality, I ended up taking out a bank loan. Fortunately, it was relatively easy to obtain, as I worked in the IT industry and had been a long-time taxpayer.

After purchasing the house, we did some renovations to make it truly our own. Finally, we were ready to move in. It was a dream come true. The feeling of unlocking the door to our new home for the first time, knowing that this space was ours, brought an overwhelming sense of accomplishment and joy.

You might wonder why, despite my initial stance against taking loans with interest, I ended up doing so. This was an emotional decision driven by my mother's wishes and mine. The house met all our needs: it was near schools, a mosque, and markets, and I could work from home.

Only those people who have lived or are currently living in a rented house will understand the struggle. We don't always get a house that meets our preferences, and we often need to relocate based on the owner's demands. There's also the constant pressure to pay rent on time, even if it means sacrificing other necessities, like food. On the other hand, the satisfaction of owning a house is immense. However, as per religious practices, taking a loan with interest is not acceptable. I pray our Creator accepts my apologies for this.

In the face of this dilemma, I started saving diligently, cutting unnecessary expenses, and focusing on repaying the loan as quickly as possible. By God's grace, I managed to repay the loan within five years. Since then, I have been living loan-free, experiencing the true freedom and peace that come with financial independence.

Now, you might think that I haven't achieved anything big, like running a successful business or building a billion-dollar company. That's true. However, my goals were different. I wanted to provide my family with a better future and ensure my kids received a good education. I aimed to secure a house for us to live in, create a happy and peaceful life, and generate some passive income. My focus was on building a substantial fund for my children's education and marriage, as well as ensuring a comfortable retirement for myself.

I've managed to achieve all these goals. I've made an impact in my family and my community by prioritizing these important aspects of life. While I may not have achieved traditional definitions of success, like becoming a business mogul, I've succeeded in creating a stable and fulfilling life for my loved ones. This accomplishment means everything to me. What else could I possibly need?

This journey reinforced the importance of perseverance and faith. As Henry David Thoreau once said, "Go confidently in the direction of your dreams. Live the life you have imagined." Striving for our goals, even when faced with challenges, can lead to incredible outcomes. Our dream of owning a home came true because we believed in it and worked tirelessly towards it. Remember, every effort you make towards your dreams brings you one step closer to realizing them. Stay hopeful, stay persistent, and trust in the journey.

Quranic Inspiration:

"Indeed, Allah is with those who are patient." (Quran 2:153)

Explanation: This verse highlights the importance of patience. Throughout the loss of my mother, navigating a new job during the pandemic, and finally purchasing our dream home, patience was a crucial element. It's a reminder that Allah supports and is with those who remain patient through life's trials.

Motivational Quote:

"The best way to predict your future is to create it." — Peter Drucker

Explanation: This quote encapsulates the proactive approach I took during challenging times. By persevering through loss, adapting to new job roles, and working towards purchasing a home, I actively created a better future for my family. It's a reminder that we have the power to shape our future through our actions.

Questions for Reflection:

1. How do you manage your finances to achieve long-term stability and security?
2. What steps do you take to ensure your family's well-being and future prosperity?
3. How do you balance saving for the future with enjoying the present?
4. What role do financial planning and education play in your life?

Summary

Losing my mother was the saddest moment of my life. Her sudden passing left a void, and I had to step up to manage the family's expenses. We decided to move to a new home to help us cope.

The COVID-19 pandemic hit hard, reducing my salary by 20-30%. To support my family, I had to withdraw my PF balance. Despite the challenges, I continued making Power BI YouTube videos and eventually landed a new job with a 250% salary hike, fulfilling my long-held dream of working in the IT sector.

This achievement taught me the importance of perseverance. I later bought a house, fulfilling my mother's dream. Though I had to take a bank loan, I managed to repay it within five years. This journey reinforced the value of resilience and faith in achieving our goals.

LAST WORD : CONCLUSION

As I come to the end of sharing my journey with you, I want to reflect on the central theme that has guided my life: "Iron does not rust alone" Just as iron deteriorates due to external forces, we too are shaped by our surroundings. Our growth or decline is shaped by the people we surround ourselves with and the environment we choose to live in.

Throughout my life, resilience has been my constant companion. From facing financial struggles to overcoming rejections, every challenge was a stepping stone to personal growth. The Quranic verse, "Indeed, with hardship [will be] ease" (Quran 94:6), perfectly encapsulates this idea. Every difficulty I encountered was followed by ease, reinforcing my belief that perseverance and faith are essential in navigating life's challenges.

One of the most significant lessons I learned was the importance of not giving up, no matter how tough the circumstances. Winston Churchill's words, "Success is not final, failure is not fatal; it is the courage to continue that counts," resonate deeply with my experiences. Every failure was an opportunity to learn and grow, and every success was a reminder to stay humble and keep pushing forward.

Faith has been my anchor. Trusting in our Creator's plan and seeking His guidance helped me navigate numerous challenges. The Hadith, "Tie your camel and trust in Allah" (Sunan al-Tirmidhi), emphasizes the importance of taking action while having faith in Allah. This teaching guided me through various stages of my life, reminding me that while I should trust in our Creator, I must also take the necessary steps to achieve my goals.

My family has been my bedrock. My mother's teachings and unwavering support provided the foundation for my values and resilience. The Hadith, "The best of you are those who are best to their families" (Sunan al-Tirmidhi), underscores the importance of family in our lives. My family's support, especially my mom's and wife's, was instrumental in my personal and professional growth. Their belief in me kept me motivated, even during the toughest times.

Adaptability is crucial in today's fast-paced world. My journey involved numerous transitions, from changing jobs and learning new skills to moving from a joint family to a nuclear family. The ability to adapt to these changes was essential for my growth. Charles Darwin's quote, "It is not the strongest of the species that survive, nor the most intelligent, but the one most responsive to change," highlights the importance of adaptability. Embracing change and being open to new opportunities allowed me to navigate life's uncertainties successfully.

Learning is a lifelong journey. The Hadith, "Whoever treads a path seeking knowledge, Allah will make easy for him the path to Paradise" (Sahih Muslim), inspired me to continually seek knowledge and improve myself. Whether it was learning new technologies, developing new skills, or understanding financial management, continuous learning was a key driver of my success.

One of the most impactful decisions I made was to start a YouTube channel on Power BI. Despite the initial struggles and slow growth, I remained committed to sharing my knowledge. This endeavor not only helped others but also reinforced my understanding and expertise. Steve Jobs said, "The only way to do great work is to love what you do." This passion kept me energized, even if it meant waking up early or staying up late to complete my work.

Community involvement and giving back were significant aspects of my journey. Contributing to the Power BI community and helping others with their queries brought immense satisfaction. The Quranic verse, "The example of those who spend their wealth in the way of Allah is like a seed [of grain] that sprouts seven ears; in every ear there are a hundred grains" (Quran 2:261), emphasizes the rewards of giving back. Helping others not only brought me recognition, such as the MVP award from Microsoft, but also reinforced the importance of community and support.

Losing my mother was one of the most challenging moments of my life. Her sudden passing left a void that was hard to fill. However, her teachings and the values she instilled in me continued to guide me. The Quranic verse, "Allah does not burden a soul beyond that it can bear..." (Quran 2:286), provided comfort and strength during this difficult time. It reminded me that every challenge is within our capacity to overcome, even when it feels insurmountable.

Moving to a new home and adjusting to life without my mother was a significant transition. It was a reminder that life is transient and that we must cherish every moment with our loved ones. The Hadith, "The strong man is not the one who wrestles well, but the strong man is the one who controls himself when he is in a fit of rage" (Sahih Bukhari), taught me the importance of emotional strength and patience during times of loss.

Financial management was a crucial aspect of my journey. Learning about personal finance, investing in mutual funds, and planning for the future were essential for securing my family's well-being. The teachings of financial experts like Ankur Warikoo and Pranjal Kamra offered valuable insights that guided me through financial challenges. I am grateful for them.

Eleanor Roosevelt's words, "The future belongs to those who believe in the beauty of their dreams," inspired me to keep dreaming and planning for a better future. Setting financial goals, saving diligently, and making informed investment decisions were key strategies that helped me achieve financial stability.

One of the most significant milestones was purchasing our dream home. This achievement was a testament to years of hard work, sacrifice, and perseverance. It fulfilled my mother's greatest wish and provided a sense of security and stability for my family. The Quranic verse, "And whoever fears

Allah – He will make for him a way out. And will provide for him from where he does not expect" (Quran 65:2-3), resonated deeply with this accomplishment. Trusting in Allah's plan and working diligently led to the realization of this dream.

Achieving this milestone didn't mean the end of my journey. It was a reminder to set new goals and continue striving for personal and professional growth. Albert Schweitzer's quote, "Success is not the key to happiness. Happiness is the key to success. If you love what you are doing, you will be successful," perfectly encapsulates the essence of my journey. Finding joy in the process and loving what you do are crucial for long-term success and fulfillment.

Why Iron Does Not Rust Alone: The Chemistry Behind It

Iron is a strong metal that we use in many things, from buildings to cars. But if you've ever seen an old, rusty nail, you know that iron can also rust. Rust makes iron weak and crumbly. But here's the key point: iron doesn't destroy itself. It's the rust that does the damage, and rust only happens because of certain conditions in the environment. Let's explore why.

The Rusting Process

Rust forms when iron reacts with oxygen and water. Imagine leaving a piece of iron outside. When it rains or the air is humid, water meets iron. Oxygen in the air is also involved. These two things – water and oxygen – start a chemical reaction with the iron. This reaction creates rust, which is a flaky, reddish-brown substance.

How Does Rust Form?

Rusting is similar to a tiny battery functioning on the surface of the iron. Different spots on the iron act like tiny electrical parts. Some areas lose iron atoms and become the anodes. The lost iron atoms leave behind electrons. These electrons travel to other spots on the iron, called cathodes, where they help oxygen from the air react with water. This whole process creates iron oxide, which is rust.

The Role of Water and Oxygen

Rusting requires both water and oxygen. If you keep iron dry, it won't rust easily because the reaction can't start without water. This is why iron objects kept indoors don't rust as quickly as those left outside in the rain. The water acts like a bridge, helping the oxygen in the air to react with the iron.

Environmental Influences

Some environments make iron rust faster. For example, if there's salt in the water (like seawater), rusting speeds up. Saltwater conducts the tiny electric currents that accelerate rusting more efficiently. That's why things made of iron, like ships or cars, rust faster near the sea.

Why Iron Itself Doesn't Destroy

Iron in its natural, pure state doesn't rust by itself. It's the water and oxygen in the environment that cause rust. If you could put a piece of iron in a place with no water and no oxygen, it would stay shiny and strong forever. So, the iron itself isn't being destroyed; rather, the rust, caused by environmental factors, leads to the damage.

Preventing Rust

With this knowledge, we can take steps to prevent rust. People often coat iron with paint or other materials to keep water and oxygen away. Sometimes, a layer of another metal, like zinc, which doesn't rust as easily, is applied to iron. This process is called galvanizing.

The Life Lesson

Our environment influence us, just like iron does. If we surround ourselves with negative influences, we might find our 'potential' getting rusty. This metaphor perfectly aligns with the central theme of my book.

Think of your mind and spirit as if they were iron. When exposed to the right conditions – positive people, healthy environments, and constructive habits – we remain strong and resilient. But if we allow negativity, toxic relationships, and bad habits to seep into our lives, it's like exposing iron to water and oxygen. Slowly, the rust forms, and our potential starts to deteriorate.

The chemistry of rusting offers a profound lesson about life. Just as we protect iron from rust by keeping it dry and covered, we need to shield ourselves from negativity by choosing our environments and relationships wisely. Surrounding ourselves with growth-minded, supportive individuals can prevent the 'rust' of negativity from forming on our potential.

In my journey, as shared throughout this book, I faced numerous challenges and setbacks. But each experience taught me the importance of maintaining a positive mindset and environment. From overcoming financial struggles to pursuing my dreams in the face of adversity, I learned that our surroundings and the people we interact with play a crucial role in shaping our success.

The most crucial role in shaping a child's future lies with the parents. It's their responsibility to instill life lessons during the early stages. Just like a building with a strong foundation can withstand a tornado, a child with a solid grounding in values and principles can face life's challenges confidently. If you are a parent, ensure that you provide your children with proper guidance and life lessons. Monitor their behavior as they grow, guiding them through different phases of life. Remember, parenting doesn't end when children reach adulthood; it's a lifelong commitment to nurturing and supporting them, ensuring they become resilient and responsible individuals.

By keeping positive influences and protecting ourselves from negativity, we can stay strong and reach our full potential. Remember, the iron itself isn't being destroyed; rather, it's the rust, caused by environmental factors, that leads to the damage. Similarly, we can safeguard our well-being by being mindful of the influences around us.

Embrace this lesson in your own life. Be vigilant about your environment and the company you keep. Just as iron can stay strong and resilient with proper care, you too can achieve greatness by nurturing a positive, supportive environment around you.

Thank you for joining me on this journey. I hope that my story inspires you to persevere through your challenges, trust in your abilities, and strive for your dreams – please do remember me in your valuable prayers. I also want to extend my heartfelt gratitude to my friends Niaz and Rafi for their unwavering support throughout my journey.

Above all, I am deeply thankful to our Creator for guiding me through every step of my life, providing strength in times of adversity, and blessing me with countless opportunities. His continuous support and wisdom have been my anchor, and I trust that He will continue to guide me in the future.

Remember, 'The only limit to our realization of tomorrow is our doubts of today' (Franklin D. Roosevelt). Believe in yourself, embrace change, and keep moving forward.

———————————

Disclaimer

The stories, experiences, and reflections shared in this book are based on the author's personal journey and perspectives. The intention is to provide insights, inspiration, and guidance through the author's life lessons and observations. While every effort has been made to ensure the accuracy of the information presented, the author and publisher make no representations or warranties of any kind regarding the completeness, accuracy, reliability, or suitability of the content.

The book also includes references to Islamic teachings, Quranic verses, and Hadiths. These references are included to provide spiritual and motivational context based on the author's understanding and interpretation. Readers are encouraged to seek additional scholarly resources for a deeper understanding of Islamic teachings.

The strategies, advice, and opinions expressed in this book are the author's own and should not be construed as professional or financial advice. Readers are encouraged to consult with appropriate professionals before making any significant decisions based on the content of this book.

The author and publisher shall not be held liable for any loss or damage, directly or indirectly, arising from the use or reliance on the information contained in this book. The reader assumes full responsibility for their own actions and decisions.

This book is intended to inspire and motivate readers. It is not a substitute for professional guidance or counseling in any area, including but not limited to financial, legal, medical, or psychological matters.